Token Woman:
The One That Got Away

J.H. Raichyk, Ph.D.

Penelope Press
Fairfield, Ohio

COPYRIGHT © 1998 By J. H. RAICHYK, Ph.D.

Published by:
T.E.Shaw
Penelope Press,
An Imprint of Dectiré Publishing
Fairfield, Ohio

All rights reserved. No part of this book may
be reproduced or transmitted in any form
or by any means, electronic or mechanical,
including photocopying, recording, or
by any information storage and retrieval system,
without permission in writing from the author,
except for the inclusion of brief quotations
in a review.

First Printing 1998
Printed in the United States of America

Library of Congress Cataloging in Publication Data
Raichyk, J. H.
Token Woman: The One That Got Away /
by J. H. Raichyk, Ph.D.

p. cm.

1. Feminism
2. Motherhood and Work
3. Decision Support - Early History of
4. Women and Technology
5. Autobiography

305.42R   1997   97-69622
LCCN
ISBN 0-9661022-5-8: $11.95 Softcover

Acknowledgements

This book owes its existence to my children for many reasons. To my son for his encouragement to try new things, to my daughter for her inspiration, support and example, I owe thanks. But even more, they were the justification behind this preoccupation with an otherwise self-regardant exercise.

The realization that they were approaching their own milestones in young adulthood and would soon be making commitments to careers and lifestyles was the beginning of the book's inception. As I realized how little on the horizon would lead to any future scenario of promise in their lifetimes, and how uninspired or untruthful were the resources young people had to rely on for guidance, I began to wonder whether any of the trials our generation struggled through had produced anything of benefit for our children. Or was it partly that those actually 'at the front' were simply too busy to write 'the dispatches'?

One path women are exploring, home-based self-employment, was showing promise and being adopted by growing numbers. Bits and pieces of data from theorists, futurists and researchers seemed to suggest to me that there was more potential here for all. But the momentum of our current direction in seeking well-being, namely corporate parity, is so overwhelming that resistance to the 'job-route' was unimaginable to many. It seemed the only way to turn the tide to a path with future promise was for our generation to expose the reasons why further effort along the old paths was so unworth pursuing as to be repugnant to our children's sensibilities. Having witnessed some of those reasons from a privileged position, I felt some responsibility and in the tradition of an explorer's narrative, have attempted to capture our adventure in this book.

Along the way I have enlisted and been the beneficiary of the generous support of several who either read, listened, promoted, made suggestions or provided contacts. Among this group are my former mentor Kenneth G. Harris, who read the manuscript for textual accuracy and Susan M. Duncan whose suggestions and evaluations were much appreciatied. Also my sister Betty Sandoz, Judith B. Gee, Alice Fosset, Elaine Stenger, Lynn Robbins, Pamela McCorduck, and the members of our teen writers' group were very helpful when called on. To them I owe thanks for taking time from their busy schedules to supply pieces for my puzzle. But, as always with the responsibility for content, ' the buck stops here'.

J.H.Raichyk, Ph.D.

Table of Contents

Prologue 1

Chapter 1 9
Credibility

Chapter 2 ...20
Computers, Calculators and Attitudes

Chapter 3 ...25
Ratemaking

Chapter 4 ...47
Stochastic Serendipity

Chapter 5 ...59
Decision Trees

Chapter 6 ...67
Twelve Month Moving Premonitions

Chapter 7 ...77
Claims and Risk

Chapter 8 ...90
MAU & Quantifying Unquantifiable Regrets

Chapter 9 ...95
The Climate and Which Way The Wind Blew

Chapter 10 ..107
Bayesian Underwriting and Commercial Fires

Chapter 11 ..116
Mathematical Models or My Kingdom for a Lotus

Chapter 12 ..130
All Good Things

Prologue

We had wagered our futures, and the futures of those who needed us, on this strange new life, this experiment in liberation. Many still do, though I wonder if they yet see it as a gamble.

In the current world, the concept had barely been tested by a few for long periods and, during the old war, by more for a short while. Not all the results were appealing. But neither was the old regime. And so, the magnetism of curiosity, was all that drew us in the beginning. It was an experiment that seemed worthy of a second look, and maybe another. Failure, they said, would bring us back to the old way. What did we have to lose?

By the time my tale begins none of us were complete neophytes in the business of living on the fringes of our world. Each had opened doors few before us had dared and each had the bruises to show for it. My doors had led through graduate

Token Woman: The One That Got Away

school to a doctoral degree in math, from which I had emerged into a medieval academic world that was in chaos over Vietnam, unionization and equal rights. Crisis after crisis and I found myself an immigrant in Canada. My compatriots in this story had escaped civil corruption elsewhere or had ventured into the treacherous waters of racial and ethnic diversity at home. We had survived; not always as predicted. But with each venture dared, success or mere survival, it mattered very little, our belief, or maybe our need to believe, grew stronger. Until it became routine to pick ourselves up, take the measure of where we stood and make our way toward that elusive goal beyond the horizon, seldom or never looking back; never wondering about bailing out. This route had our names on it and we now launched our hopes, with all on board, seeking that new world. This time we would taste the prosperity of the corporate world, find the havens we'd missed.

Some of the evil that threatened our venture, may have been inherent in the nature of our organization or the absence of it. Each of us was intent on being our own captain, in charge of our own, only making alliances as circumstance required. Our numbers were not large enough for the luxury of ranks and files in our parades nor did we see any logic in giving up liberty in the pursuit of liberty. There were certainly examples in very recent memory, where small and amorphous was adequate to secure liberty though they involved painful

Prologue

hostilities and considerations of territory. On days of optimism, we only needed to avoid direct confrontation, build consensus, make ourselves needed. Yet even then the prospect of failure was so palpable, the sense of impotence so bitter that our little cluster gradually formed ever stronger bonds.

Some have said that our problems were endemic to our generation; that those who were young in the 60's were somehow different and they point to the Vietnam resistance, the civil rights work, and the ERA as either proof or source of the problem. This virus hidden in our generation is supposed to have derailed our maturation and to have made us distrustful, even of ourselves. As a result they say we avoid responsibility and blame, depend on consensus; we're insecure, they say.

Somehow the impossibility of what's being attempted is never discussed. Is it because it's not seen? Can no one see that the Emperor stands naked? Or maybe Emperors are supposed to look that way and no one told us? Our generation has no problem with honest nudity so how come it doesn't feel right? Does that make me immature? Does that make me insecure? That feeling is familiar: the scene was a small exclusive women's college.

It was expected to be another routine day near the end of our senior year at college when, out of the ordinary, all seniors were summoned to early morning assembly. As we came together, there was an ominous gloom and the dorm students

Token Woman: The One That Got Away

were exchanging haunted looks. It was not long before the Dean, with her support staff hovering around the exits, laid down their ultimatum. They demanded confessions: the culprits must be turned in or they would grant no degrees that year. None would graduate. We were stunned. They were serious.

The instructors in our professions, supposedly independent women, our church leaders could coldly threaten us with harm, doing their injustice to innocent bystanders as well. All because a few of our wilder numbers had, for as yet unknown reasons, broken curfew and escaped capture with the assistance of a couple compatriots. Broken curfew, a truly puny offense. We were incredulous.

The world crumbled and the huge ugliness that our parents had sheltered us from within the parochial schools stood glaring down at us from the stage. The very authorities who condemned civil leaders for using their vested powers to do violence to people because of the color of their skin were now going to ruin the lives of every senior because they were members of a class. Rage competed with devastation, confusion, and disbelief. No one spoke out. The logic was inescapable. If defiance provoked them to debase the precious degree we had worked four long years to earn, then the audacity of pointing out their betrayal in front of the entire class was hardly likely to turn them from their plan. Expulsion was more likely.

Prologue

But afterward, for our shame, we would destroy the school. Solemn but informal vows passed from classmate to classmate: no daughter of mine, no sister, no friend will ever suffer these halls. We may each have gone our separate ways, losing touch with our fellow victims but over the next few years, applications dropped, then enrollment dwindled. The college made adjustments to expense, to recruitment, to admissions, to no avail. The day finally came when those leaders were forced to relinquish control. Now a college, and the name, survive but it is out of the hands of our tormentors and the exclusive, all women's church college is no more. Who won?

The irony of those events could not fail to register. We had known our liberation could not be achieved at the expense of our men: our sons were our children too. There is no joy, no liberation in losing your child to simplify the success of some -ism, no matter which cause, how vital or how grand. We would have to struggle for one male heart at a time. We had also known the majority of women did not yet support or even sympathize. And among those who sympathized many were unable to stand with us, their independence too costly. These, we thought, would need social institutions to insulate them from the injuries inflicted in their isolation. But now we stood victims of our own: our own leaders in several dimensions. We would have to be our own captains, no automatically friendly population, not even solidarity from our supposed leaders. We

Token Woman: The One That Got Away

were truly alone in our quest, our insecurity earned, but we would not abandon the experiment.

Before we have lost the collective memory of the time before the experiment began, as we have with public schooling, we should gather the stories. This narrative is clearly personal, a collage of memories. Some people store their memories in chronologies, some by content. I am one of the latter and my story is so organized but, curiously, I find that the content preserves the basic chronology of the events. I have not attempted impartiality nor generalization because no detailed record was made. To that extent it may be unfair to those others to focus on one when there were many. But I cannot tell the story of those whose alliances led beyond the office; at end of day our cluster fled down separate paths. I cannot tell the stories of those who took savage pride in flaunting their difference nor those who stripped themselves of every reminder of appetites they could not totally prevent; the group that formed around me chose a middle ground, to be neither discord nor critic. Each must tell their own story.

In this story, our life was shaped by corporate needs, some so unpleasant we dreaded the sight of their forms. But they were inevitable, unavoidable these rituals. The worst of these, the need for one to judge another's worth, to make them fit the vile order, now seems so heinous, so callous, but there in the field these tasks seemed merely distasteful, even

Prologue

unimportant routine compared to the substance and schedule of our work. And when the spectre of the suffering inflicted by this process passed before our eyes, we consoled ourselves that we had done all that was humanly possible to better the results and would put the rest aside as sad unfinished business. It would be now dishonest to dwell on these as cruel and unfeeling when at the time they seemed all we could afford...and so I won't.

Nor would my story be complete without record of our rewards and pleasures. The glamour of being exotic, the tokens of affection and appreciation, the comradeship, the aesthetic beauty of our materiel, the pride and gratification are here. There were surely moments of sweeping relief or shared joys that no longer survive the passage of time in my memory just as there are terrors so horrible the mind builds walls around them. These will be necessarily missing from my account. But the sampling of our lives included in my story is reasonably representative. It is only my hope that the glamour of this strange world, the shallowest of these rewards, not induce any of my readers to sell their services in the corporate marketplace.

Beneath the skin of that world the glamour ends and you will find yourself in an environment so sterile humanity seems to come in only one size, one shape: no child, no babushka, no rebel, no teen. When push comes to shove, you will discover

Token Woman: The One That Got Away

the shackles on your freedom of thought, of time, of direction. If you persist in that world, you must choose: to be brute or to be impotent. You may think to stand against the brutish, hierarchic process, to be the diverse one, to bend the rules as cunningly as any until they are inside out. Then, if you are strong enough to survive, they will quarantine you beneath a ceiling of glass, to be consulted only by intermediaries. Or, as in this story, you may pass as one of them so convincingly that they admit you to their councils. Then you are trapped within your unclean pretense and time and the courts of law will justifiably deny your right to your children, to the rest of humanity, to those who need you, those you love.

I have tried them both now. In neither case will you find any life but intense loneliness, wondering why and where you are headed, unable to see things because your vision is split and doubled from the attempt to look through disparate mindsets. The unwholesome stress is unavoidable because the prolonged effort to maintain two faiths, two selves, is exhausting to the point of madness. And so you will see your fellows, plodding zombie-like toward no goal of their own choosing, toward someday, inflicting unending schedules of useless distractions on their hopeless existence lest they look too long and realize the trap their poor instincts vainly warned them of, slaves of the company-store as surely as any generation past.

Chapter One
Credibility

The players on the Canadian Property & Casualty Insurance scene in the 70's filled page after page in any comprehensive listing. But if the listing was compiled based on size, there were no more than a handful of large companies. These were mostly British multinationals with names like Royal, Commercial Union, and Sun Alliance. Though they dominated their Canadian territory, the relatively diminutive size of Canada's population, in total, made even the main forces, of any industry, dependent on one another or on outsiders for rare, unique or specialized resources.

This was particularly true of insurance because so much of their nature is involved with chance, probability, statistics. In order to have meaningful data on the wide variety of risks to be underwritten, the Canadians pooled their data in a single entity, the Insurance Bureau of Canada, affectionately known as the IBC, which then made the combined analyses available

Token Woman: The One That Got Away

to each member of the pool. Although this made their information functioning viable, it severely hampered their competitive urges.

Whatever benefit a company might think would accrue to it because of its perceptive underwriting practices or its expeditious claims handling or its sleek operations or its inspired marketing, they had no statistically justifiable way to alter the industry pooled rates and target more profitable growth to reward their pains. And so the entire industry marched to practically the same tune. That is, until the mid-70s when the largest companies were reaching a size sufficient to stand, statistically, more on their own.

Convinced that they should no longer be so dependent on those who were not their peers, these major players became restless to go their own way, each of them suspicious that the other would make the move first and gain some irretrievable advantage. Each monitored the others' movements, impending movements, even gossip on improved record keeping, hiring, group compliance at the IBC. The main difficulty that kept one and all from bolting from the IBC, was the fact that there was only one Property & Casualty Actuary in all of Canada and he resided at the IBC, under the watchful eyes of the entire industry.

Having an Actuary of your own was the key to independence. Not only did you need to be able to assess the masses of data required for ratemaking, you also needed to convince provincial regulators that your shining new rating structure based, in some mysterious way on your own numbers and producing presumably significantly different rates than your competitors, was legitimate, defensible. Not just any actuary would do either. The garden variety actuary, the life actuary, had very little exposure to the complexity of data characteristic of the Property & Casualty industry. More than half of their training was irrelevant to the computations of non-life risk. This, of course, did not mean that a life actuary could not do those computations, merely that his credentials were not the desired ones. The Restless Ones discounted the life actuary solution, except as a short-term solution.

Their candidate of choice, especially when the long-term perspective was their concern, would have to be a genuine, imported Property & Casualty Actuary. But the nearest source, the states to the South, turned out to be prohibitively expensive. Actuaries there usually were ranked quite high in the corporate structure, insisted on avoidance of Canadian taxation, and had substantial moving expenses. The prospects of luring an import, within any reasonable budget, was infinitesimal. That left only slower, more arduous alternatives and each knew that the others would arrive at the same conclusion.

Commercial Union, one of the multi-nationals, secured

Token Woman: The One That Got Away

approval from home office in London to pursue that next most viable route: finding local talent willing to be trained, as quickly as possible, to become their in-house winged beast. They would create a new department to be called Underwriting Analysis, headed by their most senior underwriter. The position would be titled simply, Analyst, but the requirements would be Actuarial-Trainee-without-Trainer/Fast-Learner. To carry out the search as expeditiously as possible, they would use an outside agency, an open invitation to industry gossip, knowing that whatever their competitors concluded would not advance those outside speculations beyond what each competitor should have already figured.

By sheer coincidence on my part, I had picked up a brochure in the campus library, a year and a half before, that described the actuarial profession in terms that sounded Merlin-esque, my oldest dream. Dreams are something you live off when you are an immigrant. Very few were the jobs there in the early 70's without the fine print that said 'minimum two years Canadian experience'. Not too surprising, considering the number of young people from the states to the south who, like us, had recently, simply come to stay, making more and more Canadians feel somewhat claustrophobic. Our two years was more than half over but my horizon seemed unchanged. The academic job I had managed to land had no future, the job market in my field was still in the state of collapse, and

Credibility

though I had managed to publish my doctoral dissertation, the response was truly underwhelming. So I had been cruising the career shelves.

It may seem a little late to be career shopping but up to the year before my graduation, the job market for mathematicians had been very promising. With the war ending and the demise of the aerospace industry my career prospects were not going to get brighter any time soon.

Nor were Yitz's. My husband had been an Israeli paratrooper, delaying his education and vocational choices. Our whirlwind relationship had been as colorful as Yitz's past. In all the turmoil Yitz seemed unable to get his bearings at all, which put that much more pressure on my ability to navigate the salaried world. Our marriage lived very close to the rocks on some days.

On other days dreams buoyed us. The delight of watching our precious son discover the world was the only constant beacon. Never having experienced the realities of daycare before, I couldn't believe how hard it had been to leave Michael each day. The callousness of some daycare managers was only overshadowed by the horror of strangeness, pandemonium and glare that suggested mazes and warehousing instead of home. How could a child not feel abandoned there? 'Of course they cry at first,' one assured me, standing in the play area surrounded by kennel-like chain link fence. 'But

13

Token Woman: The One That Got Away

that's natural; they stop after a little while,' was added, helpfully? My inner voice hissed that measles were just as natural but not what any mother would desire for her child. Not at least in my experience, not in my mother's house, not among my friends at college. Resignation, loss of hope, and simple exhaustion were tribute to those children's intelligence, their pain or psychological disfigurement. What were the costs they could not tell us any other way? And likely wouldn't later realize were not their ancestors' heritage.

Even after we found a smaller, newly opened site with experienced, caring nannies in the babies' room and an extremely low initial child-to-nanny ratio, the leaving was difficult. My mind was frequently so preoccupied with anxiety over Michael's understanding and how long this pseudo-satisfactory situation would last, and it didn't, that one morning in my distracted haste I ran across the road, oblivious to the oncoming traffic. The shock was enough to put me back on alert but it did nothing to diminish the loss I felt. The incredible impatience to traverse the distance instantaneously on my way back from classes summoned intense desires for telepathy to re-establish our connection. This was not my expectation of how motherhood would feel.

At least when the noise from Yitz's latest personal crash had dimmed and I had convinced him to take over daycare for those few hours, I knew Michael was in no distress

Credibility

while I was at work. The daycare nightmare was then temporarily over and I had hopes that if the reprieve would last another year or two, maybe Michael would be old enough to feel comfortable in daycare when I was at work. Then all we needed, or so I thought, was to get on our feet financially. In the meantime we had occasional help from my Mother, though she and I never talked about how bad it was when Yitz's temper was loose. That was my problem only.

Searching for a new career in those pamphlets had been less than pleasant until I discovered this whole new world that sounded so exciting, conjuring images of mathematical wizardry in the service of kings who provided their subjects with the protection of financial stability in the face of life's unexpected injuries. Best of all, the route to this vision of Camelot was not out of my way. There was a sequence of tests that you studied for, on your own time, of which I had none, but the first two exams covered material I taught in my work at the university. Over half of the exams were mathematical in concept and the remaining material you were expected to encounter in your trainee workdays on the job. Somewhere between operations research and mathematical economics, the concepts the actuary was supposed to invoke in practice, had been closer to my undergraduate dreams than the elegant abstractions of my dissertation. It was a dream where I felt at home, at last.

Testing day came the following spring and I aced the

Token Woman: The One That Got Away

first two exams. Celebration was not in order though because Yitz crashed badly the same day my results arrived. In any event my timing was too early. The personnel department of each company I approached seemed baffled at the mention of my intended career choice. By the end of the second week of calling, I abandoned the search. Like many real dreams, this one had developed an air of incredibility. None of them knew what an actuary was! Stunned, I couldn't imagine what had gone wrong. So I signed on for another year of academic life, and want ads.

By the following spring, Yitz had found an intensive, but short-term, career oriented educational program and I had decided that my only chance to find my way on the Canadian scene was to consult an agency. I had barely returned from that first meeting when the agent called with an interview for a position that could lead to the actuary's chair at the third largest insurer in Canada, hinting that there was another major company that might compete for me. The world went from resignation and backdoors to limelight and suitors.

Preparing for the interview, I tried to keep my expectations under control, reminding myself that this job, which was not in my pocket yet, would be entry level. The visual cues as I entered the financial district in Toronto reawakened my Camelot. It was impossible to approach those sleek, black steel and impeccably polished marble towers,

Credibility

wherein resided my intended employer, without seeing modern castles, decked in many colored flags and overlooking majestic canyons with an actual lake that sprawled into the distance. Inside the sedate offices of Commercial Union Assurance, there was no avoiding the comparison with the grungy classroom. The bottom of this ladder was an immediate improvement.

Waiting to meet Mr. Atkinson, head of Underwriting Analysis, who personnel had told me would be my boss in this venture, I wondered how I would convince him that I was the right candidate for winged beast. Three years in purgatory had almost convinced me that I was an impostor. Still, I felt curiously at ease as I scanned my surroundings, calm, tasteful modestly British. Moments later Colin Atkinson entered, an absolute vision of an aging knight, veteran of many battles. His underwriting credentials were substantial but his role recently was more in the line of ambassador, negotiator. He was the company's representative to the IBC, had actively worked on ratemaking committees with their actuary and was becoming a major force in the development of the industry-wide pool, the Facility, for uninsurable drivers.

Our discussion was pleasant but unremarkable until we rose to do a tour of the offices. For some reason, my eye caught the title of a small blue pamphlet lying on the credenza and, in a moment of inspired enthusiasm, I picked it up and zeroed in on exactly what I needed...Credibility. Credibility theory,

Token Woman: The One That Got Away

actually. But the definition in the text so appealed to me with its clarity and elegance that my mathematical instincts involuntarily engaged, bringing with it the smiles and the warm glow usually reserved for baby-watching or engagement rings. The formula for the credibility of a sample had emerged from insisting that the expected square error be minimal when you're splitting the weighting between the sample, whose credibility was in doubt, and the population, which was considered solid. The credibility was that weight. It functioned so beautifully; it was so intuitively natural, the credibility weighting for the sample increased when the sample size increased and/or when the relative variability of the sample decreased. It was lovely! But best of all, when the situation involved estimating frequencies, there was a classic approximation theorem, Chebyshev's, that revealed the real nature of the concept. Credibility was a limiting relationship between the sample size needed and a specified probability that the actual frequency be within a given interval around the estimate. The clarity of this probabilistic image was so exciting, the delight of sudden revelation nearly took my breath away. 'So elegantly derived.'

That's when I noticed that my host, who had paused to accommodate this unexpected interruption, was now also beginning to beam. His response that this concept was the key to using company data for ratemaking, his first priority, told

Credibility

me I had scored. His warmth was not mere contagion, but acknowledgement of my credibility.

Token Woman: The One That Got Away

Chapter Two
Computers, Calculators and Attitudes

Never having lived within the walls of Corporate Canada before, I was intrigued with this new world. Everything was so tidy and controlled; not at all like campus with its turmoil, masses of students constantly moving, floods of them at intervals, thousands of nameless faces, some boisterous, most just trudging to their next appointment. No graffiti, no noise, no chatting, refreshments promptly at teatime, an air of privacy and respect for the work in progress.

The group of chiefs was barely a handful. One vice-president, plain vanilla. Plus a handful of managers distributed through the provinces. The rest were indians. The chiefs had all risen slowly through the ranks, the youngest with almost twenty years seniority. The indians seemed to revere the vast storehouse of history that their chiefs had acquired through many lateral moves, great familiarity with every aspect of their areas and wide arrays of contacts. That eliminated schoolish competition, with its sense of hollow victory; that destructive jumping of hoops to please some momentary authority, that passing of one test on a subject with some unknown element of luck, possibly, and then moving to some new chapter, some other unfamiliar assessor. Respect for the chiefs came naturally because it was earned. Their authority was based on their knowledge and performance, not some clever career move, some non-intrinsic patronage, some appearance, nor some ticking clock.

The small number of chiefs also made their territories fairly clearly defined and encouraged team playing. Among the chiefs themselves, there was this acknowledgement of each other's expertise. They were confident in those finely honed skills, those instincts they could count on and would need from one another. Because this process was considered the right way, the way that everyone expected to go through, the chiefs then had more respect and consideration for their indians. At least that was the impression I gathered, watching their transactions, and I had an excellent view of this land because the winged beast was to live among the chiefs.

As the winged-beast-to-be, I was an exception in several ways. The most obvious difference was that I was young and female. It took a bit of exploring the honeycomb of offices before I realized that I was the only one, except secretaries, who fit that description. Not that it mattered

Token Woman: The One That Got Away

much to me. Since the days of graduate school, I had become accustomed to those proportions without viewing myself as a minority or under-privileged.

In fact, what had worried me more in graduate school was that being female gave me some undue advantage making it hard for me to be sure, on some days, that I was as good as my results seemed to show. Even though I was very careful, without becoming paranoid, not to give anyone reason to accuse me of this unearned benefit, there had been one time when that spectre had really ambushed me. My thesis adviser, whom I admired for his tough standards, had admitted, under manipulation by a social worker in a sensitivity workshop, that maybe he was tougher on his male students. I was stunned. I hadn't seen any evidence of that and told myself that he had succumbed to pressure tactics, but from that day on he never fully regained my trust.

At C.U. my concern was that I was the only green one in insurance matters and there was no way I would ever be able to match the chiefs in that arena. My goal instead was to become literate: conversant in their jargon and knowledgeable in the area of their mathematical and data tools. Every encounter, however minor, became an opportunity to observe attitudes, catalog data sources, query procedures. The atmosphere was very purposeful and sedate so I wondered if they might be impatient but they accepted my presence without alarm

Computers, Calculators & Attitudes

because I was rumoured to know esoteric things about their data and because of their self-confidence. Or maybe because I was a young woman appealing to their paternal instincts? Besides they saw I was as cautiously curious about what they did and what it meant to them as they were about winged beasts.

What I learned was that they revered data integrity and knew, from intimate acquaintance, just how tainted every source was. Gauging the magnitude of the unseen components in each data source based on their extensively trained instincts, they wisely preferred the undisturbed sources to unknown improvements. Appropriate to the roughness of their data, was the roughness of their tools. Although most had a basic calculator on their desk, calculations were doublechecked with pencil and paper, partly for documentation purposes. One of the more conservative chiefs was rumoured to take the attitude that he was checking 'that' machine, rather than simply confirming that all data had been entered correctly, which greatly amused my mentor and boss. It amused me too, that is, until I realized that our conservative friend was truly reflecting the very loyal preference for an astronaut-guided landing over a computer-guided one.

Though they were not eager, they were open to new possibilities if those ideas offered insight or workload relief. Those would be my keys. Long experience had made them skeptical of trendiness without productivity that would benefit

Token Woman: The One That Got Away

their indians. The prospect of some computerization of the vast amounts of paperwork that went on in the branches, as well as some accounting functions, had already stirred their imaginations. Even though it was seen as beneficial to their branch personnel in the long run, <u>if</u> it delivered the paperwork savings it promised, they were concerned about how they would be able to deal with the discontinuity in their data, as well as the disruption the changeover would inflict on their staff. But most of all, they had been infinitely careful to ensure that it wouldn't eliminate any of their indians. The chiefs and indians <u>were </u>the company, not some abstract entity of legal creation nor some stock market conglomerate of investors; the indians were clearly assets which the chiefs sought to develop, using the company resources to assist their indians to perform; all of which demonstrated to me clearly that this new world was very tribal.

Chapter Three
Ratemaking

Our first and primary objective in Underwriting Analysis was to calculate automobile insurance rates that would reflect the company's own claims results. In preparation, I studied every IBC example in our files and queried the chiefs in other underwriting areas about their ratemaking processes. Apparently automobile was the only area in which we would apply actuarial practices and those practices seemed very formal. The results, however, would be anything but cut and dried.

In the world of Property & Casualty the inhabitants subscribed to one of two mindsets. There were those who saw the rates as a process of developing histories, balancing statistical considerations and forecasting the future. Especially forecasting the future. They were acutely aware of the fact that even the most recent history available to base our rates on was for policies written more than a year before and

Token Woman: The One That Got Away

needed to be projected a long way through the mists. They struggled to see beyond the date of approval and implementation, beyond the twelve months those rates would be used in the market place, beyond the twelve months after that when the last covered accident of the last policy sold in this planned year would occur, and even thirty months beyond that when those last claims would be sufficiently along the process of being paid and closed to be considered complete. Until then, they would not know whether the premiums calculated in this ratemaking exercise had been adequate to produce a profit for the company. Their calendar had sixty months.

    To improve their aim, they carefully studied several years of claims history, looking for trends in frequency, in severity, in the patterns of payment, in the adequacy, over time, of reserving practices for the unpaid portion of claims. They pondered over what sort of events might cause shifts in those trends. Would the public tire of safety features in the cars they drove, would law enforcement become lax in the areas they felt were the leading causes of accidents, would the economy force changes in driving patterns, would the government be able to contain the inflation rates, would the courts award even larger settlements? They put their fingers in the air, or tried to remember situations that felt as dire, and how much those past crises actually moved their earlier results. Their soothsayers were gloomy and felt the company needed to move the rates up rapidly.

The other group lived by the taxman's calendar, the shareholders' laws. Their focus was on this twelve months, here and now, the premiums written in them and the claims reported in them. Every day was spent dealing with the public, with the agency forces, with the taxman. They studied the competition and queried the independent agents for their assessment. Why were the premiums written this year by agents in this territory down? They watched for signs of any political movement that would impact their bookkeeping. They wanted to scoop the competition, they wanted to have good news to appease the agency powers. They feared a different trend, one in which the agents stopped looking at our rates when advising their clients. Market share was the key to their success. Premiums and claims reserves were simply their investment resources. Their opinion seldom matched the soothsayers' and the divergence was becoming acutely uncomfortable for the senior chiefs.

The success of the company depended on both sets of requirements being met, but was it possible? If not, should they compromise? Who was right? How would Home Office react? Having a rating structure that reflected the company's experience was hoped to be the basis for resolving the divergence. Their desired structure would lower the premium in

Token Woman: The One That Got Away

profitable areas, hopefully by more than our competition, making the twelve month inhabitants happy, while raising it for business we found unprofitable producing the premiums needed to cover those claims when the sixty months were finally clear. The new rate structure would be closely watched by the senior chiefs.

Being the actuarial trainee, I should have been among the advocates of the sixty month mindset. But I was too new to have a mindset nor any preconceived ideas about whether the ratemaking process I saw defined by the IBC would deliver our senior chiefs from their dilemma. My day-to-day proximity to the underwriting chiefs, instead of an actuary, increased my sensitivity to the twelve month mindset, somewhat, simply because the underwriters were users of both calendars. As the period approached for our first ratemaking exercises, I was more concerned with performing in the limelight of this controversy than in its resolution, however intriguing and suspenseful.

In my role as winged beast, my mentor equipped me with the latest in programmable calculators and I set out to fill the books of rates with legions of numbers to match their moons and portents. The theoretical framework for the IBC's ratemaking formulas was as intricate and fascinating as any Moorish palace and my task was to explore the company's actual data and build as much of the structure as was needed.

That required understanding the reasons behind the statistics and behind the art.

The main difficulty the structure had to overcome was the degree to which the claims data needed to be segmented. A rating program had to account for the area where the car was located, the type of car, the driver's age category and accident history as well as the coverage, whether it was bodily injury, property damage, collision, or some other risk. Since there were thousands of distinct combinations of these, handling them all at once was out of the question. Otherwise the claims data would be spread so thinly that many combinations would have little or no data on which to base even an opinion much less a justifiable estimate.

The solution was to define a rating formula, for a given type of coverage, to be the product of factors: one factor for area, one for car, one for age, one for history; to be applied to a generic premium. The generic premium for that type of claim could use all the data as its base and be that much more sound as an estimate. In this scheme the collision data, for example, would generate the collision generic premium and then would be spread across age categories only and examined: that is, each age category's experience would be measured relative to the entire collision experience to get the factor that should modify any generic collision premium to make it appropriate for a generic driver in that age category. The process would then be

Token Woman: The One That Got Away

repeated for the next factor, say area, using all the data again and producing the factors for area. And so on, for car type and history.

This solution strategy was valid, theoretically, as long as age, area, history, and car were independent; independence for age and area meant, for example, that knowing the driver's age would not predict the car's area. Always a mathematically desirable assumption, because of it's ability to simplify formulas, independence was not really unreasonable. If it had been untrue to any significant extent then using this simplification would skew the results since some dependent aspects would be multiply counted.

An appealing approach in its proposed simplicity of repetition but now its inherent Moorish intricacy began to emerge.

Setting validity aside, in most provinces the area factor remained a problem, even under this scheme of independent dimensions. Our data was still being spread into unacceptably small samples for the area factors. The real world reason was that political jurisdictions jealously insisted on being handled separately from their neighbors. Even the entire industry's data for some of those areas was inadequate to give samples that were unlikely to be unaffected by unusual patterns. Now that may seem oddly phrased to some but it was unfortunately appropriate to statistics since that branch of mathematics strives to eliminate negatives, which then requires its focus to be acutely negative. Anyway, the distortions in these small samples was not just a matter of a few flukes that could simply be discarded because disposing of one, and its opposite counterpart for balance, could then materially misstate the average by an equally unknowable amount in such small samples. In fact, in some cases it could be the absence of certain representative claim sizes that was the fluke.

The only viable way to deal with inadequate samples was to get more data. To do that meant using more years of claims history than just the most recent, or else using industry data, which was to be our last, last resort.

Staying within these constraints of maximizing the company's input, led to more Byzantine complications because claims histories, which had two dimensions of their own, frequency and size, were not static. They developed.

To be precise, claims for ratemaking were classified by their policy year: the year the policy was written being indicative of the premium charged for that business and the number of risks covered by those premiums. In a perfect world, we would know those claims we had incurred when the last of those policies expired. But in actuality there was a substantial lag in reporting claims, as well as a period of uncertainty about what they would cost so each year's claims data was at a different stage of completion. Clearly, judging claim frequency

Token Woman: The One That Got Away

or claim size based on raw history would be like trying to compare cookie recipes when some samples had not been in the oven as long as others. Some adjustment would be needed before we could combine the data and begin the grand repetitive computations.

To develop a finished history for claim frequency required that we layout the recorded history of each policy year's claims count, as we knew it at each age of its development. The resulting array would be naturally triangular, as in this example where the claims counts, at various ages, are given horizontally for each policy year listed:

	Age, in years				
Policy Year	1	2	3	4	5
1970	250	300	305	306	306
1971	200	260	263	266	
1972	250	310	317		
1973	300	380			
1974	350				

In this example, we had been tracking the oldest policy year claims the longest and their numbers had stabilized by year 5. From these claims counts, the observed year-over-year growth rates were calculated, for each policy year. The unknown portions of each policy year's history, the blank parts of the table, were then estimated by using the averages of those observed growth rates and applying them, as needed, to the last known claims count for each policy year. These projected claims counts would fill the lower triangle as shown below and the finished state of each policy year's claims would occupy the final column, age 5. Stability at last for claims count.

	Age, in years				
Policy Year	1	2	3	4	5
1970					
1971					266
1972				320	320
1973			388	391	391
1974		438	446	451	451

These fully developed claims counts in that final column would be the basis for the frequencies associated with those policy years, leaving claim size to be dealt with next.

Size, known as severity, was also affected by development. Its arabesque variations on the triangular motif no less lovely. The size was a combination of the amounts paid to date as well as an estimate of the amounts remaining to be paid. This total, though it was an indication from the beginning of the finished claim size, was inherently unstable and its movement, with its dependence on an estimate, a reserve, a budget, was not considered handsome because it was not unidirectional or consistent or even explainable.

When claims were relatively new, the process of discovery would affect how adequate the estimate was. As

Token Woman: The One That Got Away

claims aged, more of the amounts were paid so the size was less dependent on the estimate and became more stable but the total would still be moving, the direction depending on the reserving philosophy of the claims department and on how unexpected were the trends in jury settlements and inflation.

If a claim's estimate was overly optimistic then its payments would eventually exceed the budget, forcing the estimate, and of course the total, to be increased. Although the law of large numbers might smooth the swings as savings based on pessimism balanced optimism's losses, our numbers were not large and our views were not knowable so the data swung in embarrassingly erratic patterns over time. A jury settlement that went in favor of the company could make a huge reserve suddenly disappear as unnecessary. Reserving philosophy, i.e. whether the claims staff was instructed to be pessimistic or optimistic while estimating, was assumed to be constant over time, but was a total unknown. Because the movements of reserves for the unpaid part of claims were so quirky, the development patterns for size were based on the payment history only, its movement more consistent but more sedate and slow to climax.

That slowness varied considerably by type of claim. Since bodily injury claims took much longer to settle, their size development pattern was substantial and took many years. In contrast, collision took just a couple years to develop.

Ratemaking

Obviously, the first thing that had to be done in order to use more severity history was to develop all years to the same stage, that is, as soon as all payments had been inflated to current price levels. One more plot twist before denouement.

All data being fully developed, we now had apples and apples, but they were today's apples and we needed tomorrow's, so we were looking for trends. We needed to use whatever projected inflation the soothsayers felt was appropriate to convert all data from a given policy year to the price levels expected many months in the future when the claims covered by this rate structure would actually be paid. In addition, any future trends in frequency were built in now.

So how many years of history could we, or should we, use? Because the credibility of an estimate decreased as the variability of the sample increased, and because the claim size turned out to be a highly variable quantity, the number of years of company history needed for credibility on size was not likely to be available to me. Recency and age both being under curious limitations.

The most recent year available was for policies written more than a year ago because it was necessary to wait until the time periods covered by that premium had expired, i.e. the end of the year following the policy year. Adding to that the time it took the IBC to gather each company's data and process it made the phrase 'most recent year' seem annoyingly ancient.

Token Woman: The One That Got Away

Annoying because of the discipline required to constantly refocus your sense of time and because the news that fueled the gloom was happening on the street, now, and not nearly as dramatically as in the data.

Besides the limits of availability, there were also limits to how many years could be used because of irrelevance. Changes in automobile engineering, road building, medical practices, law enforcement and many other unknowables made older histories, even when available, less useful. Canadian ratemaking exercises typically used three to five years of history so that became my goal, or rather my limit.

Even with all our history, our actuarial credibility, while reaching interesting levels, still required incorporation of industry data in order to achieve full credibility. This meant repeating the entire process with industry data and then using a credibility weighted average of our data and the industry's to get the base data for each and every factor in this construction of illusions.

Using the factors generated in this process I could finally begin filling the rating tables. In practice, because of the large amount of changing data in each calculation, there were very few shortcuts available with a calculator. Allowing for error-checking as well, made the process a test of mindfulness.

Meanwhile, my mentor was attending many meetings at

the IBC to keep his finger on the pulse of the industry as their actuary calculated the IBC rates; and he frequently returned with new ideas on trends. This necessitated recalculation, virtually from scratch. When the tables would reach all the way to completion without new IBC trends, selected provinces' rates were circulated to senior chiefs for their assessment. Or rather for testing among the twelve month tribe, because the responses that my mentor returned with from these presentations was that there were some apparently critical territories where the twelve month tribe was not happy and so the structure must be re-examined, with some change of assumption.

After discarding many books of rating tables, I was convinced that a programmable calculator was not the appropriate equipment for such a game. My mentor, an obvious advocate of the stiff upper lip, seemed somewhat in the state of shock at the suggestion of computers. I wondered what victories had been required to secure approval for my fancy calculator because he was patently reluctant to even discuss adding to my resources. It became apparent after some prodding that computers were considered the extravagances of national governments and Southerners' space ventures, not the sort of expense for a junior winged beast. Probably my Southern ancestry was to blame for my poor sense of proportion.

This was not easy to argue against because in my

Token Woman: The One That Got Away

previous life as a mathematician the attitude promoted among my brethren had been that mathematicians did not calculate, sniff, sniff, we developed theories that elegantly solved problems without bloody calculations. In fact, just proving that a solution existed was felt to be the limit of our interest. It was the engineers, who needed slide rules, calculators and related paraphernalia for brute force calculating. Other than logic, my only defenses were limited. The actuarial brochure had hinted that access to computing power was not inappropriate, the IBC actuary had a computer at his disposal and I had heard rumours that the actuary in our life insurance division occasionally used one. None of these seemed persuasive though I noticed a slight wavering in my mentor's opposition at the mention of our life actuary so I resolved to pursue the issue, with or without orders.

Several phone calls to the life division made it clear that either very little use was being made of the alleged computer or its user was carefully concealing it. No one volunteered much. After deciding that the direct approach was my best chance, I simply showed up unannounced in the actuarial area of the life insurance division. Fortunately, looking purposeful was sufficient to gain access to people in the area and gradually my candidate list narrowed to a Mr. Hodge.

The man himself was much less formal than my tribe in Property & Casualty. We traded anti-IBM stories and discussed his calculations, at least the few he said he'd programmed on a little teletype terminal. Apparently he was dialing up Comshare, a time-sharing service with a behemoth of immense proportions, and writing his programs in Fortran. Well, my one exposure to computers had been a little project I had done, mostly for my amusement, as a faculty member at SUNY Brockport, in the States to the South. The computer there was jealously guarded and my initiate status confined my exposure to key-punching my cards which I then left in a designated cubicle outside the sanctuary of the elect, one of whom would then emerge at intervals, retrieve batches, and return previous batches, with output or error messages; only the elect knew how to speak to the computer and request its attention to our lowly punch card offerings. But at least the language I'd used was the right one.

My appetite now whetted, I was anxious to see this thing called a teletype terminal but it was not in his possession. It was back in the hands of its other master, none other than our own personnel tribe. He had no idea what they were doing with it, and I wondered. He reassured me the billing was simple and modest, if you were efficient. So I returned to my mentor and confidently reported that the power we sought existed here in the company and we needed only to borrow it for limited periods. No purchase was necessary, no commitment. And for such rental expenses our limited resources would

Token Woman: The One That Got Away

certainly be adequate since there were precedents, approvals of similar justifications.

My mentor seemed swayed by this favorable news. His later promise of funding was vague but what concerned me even more was the realization that I would have to learn to appease the behemoth while in alien territory. Since the personnel tribe had no programming staff, they had to have been using a canned program, possibly even linked up to a different behemoth. I could see no advantage to working in their quarters but there seemed no negotiating room left. Of all the Property & Casualty tribes, personnel was the most anti-social. It may have been a necessity for them to be in secured space but their closed door seemed to affect their attitude or at least the attitudes of the other tribes. I wasn't sure which was more intimidating: the reality of facing an unknown behemoth with precious little preparation or being an alien in the midst of paranoia.

After an inauspicious first encounter in which I learned the significance of full and half duplex the hard way, my programming skills grew to match my needs. But that first day's difficulties had drawn even more interest than I had feared. The moment the terminal had begun to stutter, some observer had sent down to the systems tribe. Whether it was territorial interest or curiosity, my would-be rescuer was not one of their indians but their chief. Nothing short of a medical emergency would have stirred so much standing about and kibitzing among the tribes. Fortunately, the rest of my session that day had been uneventful, even productive.

Like the keypunch, the teletype had effectively no editing capability or visual display worth mentioning but its operating system was a vast improvement over punchcards and allowed me to focus on the programs. Gradually I developed a prototype and began to acquire an appreciation of good design. Input and output were rough, but adequate for transfer to office formats. The most time consuming process for me was building the bases of data, especially with the limited editing inherent in the teletype. But by that time I had a new friend, with impeccable typing skills, who was eager to try her hand at this strangely animated machine. All I had to do was spring the device from its captivity in personnel for a weekend and Mary and I teamed up for our first adventure.

Soon legions of rates were marching off that teletype terminal. When the whims of chiefs or marketplace moods changed the tune, my only difficulties were access and the joys of peering down into the teletype's carriage to monitor its pulse. Gradually the dust settled and the chiefs called in a consulting actuary to legitimize our progeny. After a respectable amount of scrutiny, he was to take the rates before the various provincial boards for approval, beginning with our largest markets in Quebec and Ontario.

Token Woman: The One That Got Away

On the day I completed those volumes, my mentor returned looking grayer than usual. Word had reached the IBC that the Insurance Board in New Brunswick had called in a life actuary from the States to challenge all rate increases brought before the Board. What alarmed the insurance community and sent the news spreading like wildfire even before it was confirmed, was the fact that this particular rogue had some extravagant ideas about how to quantify frequency trends. None of my mentor's colleagues felt that they could accommodate these requirements and they expected to find their rates disallowed in the middle of the inflation crisis developing in Canada. When I heard of his cubic approximation theories, I ratified the IBC actuary's opinion that these techniques were a matter of art, a personal judgment call at best. Our chiefs fumed over the unfairness of this opponent with his unfounded demands. They realized that our consulting actuary could at best achieve a standoff if he locked horns with the rogue. With two equivalent experts at odds, the likelihood that the Board would accept our expert's version was vanishingly small. Worst of all was the possibility that the rejection would arouse the fears of other provincial boards that they were accepting unpopular rate increases when little New Brunswick had found a weakness in the rates and escaped those increases. If our rates were to endure, our chiefs would need to invent a new strategy.

Ratemaking

In the face of this feeling of impotence, they decided to postpone approaching the major provinces with our rates and focus on far-off New Brunswick. On short notice, I was asked to ride shotgun with our party and to add the weight of my testimony to our argument. In their political wisdom, they felt that my mathematical background might be seen as germane to the subject and that together with our consulting actuary and my mentor with his negotiating skills, we might be able to outflank New Brunswick's hired gun.

This was the first time my participation had ever been mentioned and I felt nonplused by this sudden attention with its reliance on credentials instead of logic. It seemed hazardous to me as my specialty in mathematics was not statistics; it had been topology, which was less relevant to the debate. When I pointed this difficulty out to my mentor, he seemed more concerned that my opinion had changed. Assured that it hadn't, he resumed his preparations for battle, scouting out who had the latest news, who would face the Board before us, and all manner of plans and strategies to be used by his counterparts in other companies. I wondered what to prepare when my instructions maintained that nothing I said would be understood.

When we arrived the evening before the presentation, my mentor again put out his feelers. By the next morning he had, among other things, acquired a copy of the questions with

Token Woman: The One That Got Away

which the Board intended to confront all insurers. There, midway down the list, was the infamous sequence on cubic estimation. My mentor impressed on me the importance of my role in demolishing the technique's credibility. Not only our rates but the rights of our colleagues to fair consideration depended on the Board's abandoning this requirement.

Braced for the worst, we waited in the gallery for a few minutes while the previous applicant finished their session. The Board members sat at tables clustered on a low dais and their actuary had a small table of his own off to one side. When Commercial Union's turn was called, my mentor took the lead and introduced our trio. It suddenly became clear to me how creative our chiefs could be. With the resonant voice of a herald he announced to all present that I was 'Dr. Raichyk, our company Statistician'. To that moment, my degree had been invisible in company affairs but now it was a flail to be used in combat and, of course, it was obvious what my specialty must be. No one would ever think to ask. I wonder if there was any sign of shock in my face as I looked around and smiled weakly in acknowledgement because at that point the atmosphere became very cordial.

With all the gallantry of Confederate gentlemen, so concerned that, being 'the only young woman among so many old gray heads', I might be distressed with the 'inquisitorial nature' of their proceedings, they offered me a seat among the

Board members so that I might feel more at home. Smiling, I, of course, graciously accepted, taking a seat in their midst with a clear view of friend and foe below.

When the flattery subsided and the questioning of our actuary began, I wondered if their hospitality changed the equation for their hired gun. I sensed that he was, for some reason, at arms length from the Board members, not fraternal at all. Did he wonder if the Board would be resolute in supporting this esoteric technique he was introducing? Wouldn't the Board be somewhat embarrassed by an idea they had no hope of understanding? Since the weakness in his approach was statistical and I couldn't believe he wasn't aware of the leap in logic he was making, he must have known why the 'company Statistician' was attending. If I could make my point without introducing hostility, would I gain the upper hand or was the brawl envisioned by my mentor inevitable? I almost felt as though I already had the upper hand and that my goal should be to retain it.

When we reached the section of the list centering on frequency worries, the gentle-member next to me turned and asked what data I might have that I would be willing to share. This looked like my chance to drive the wedge between the rogue and the Board members deeper. The request seemed reasonable and so I explored what they were hoping for and recognized a match with work I was already compiling. He

Token Woman: The One That Got Away

and his colleagues seemed pleased with my offer and the questioning continued. When the rogue reached the offensive items on the list he omitted them, totally, without comment of any kind. To me that meant we were home free. Our actuary should be able to defend our rates with reasonable ease and if the rogue attempted to reinstate those questions at other hearings, our colleagues would have our experience as a precedent. So I sat back and simply remained on guard for any return to those omitted items.

After the hearing, my mentor made it clear he did not share my level of enthusiasm, reporting glumly to our chiefs over the phone that things had not gone according to plan and we would have to await the Board's decision. He would not admit this novel idea that co-operation with the Board was better practice than his theory of conflict. He never objected to my offer of data, so he must have promised his cronies or our chiefs that we would return with the rogue's head on a platter. Without blood and destruction, he felt empty-handed; and his dour preference for direct objectives, or maybe his dislike of independent operatives taking the initiative, made our return trip chilly. In my isolation I even wondered whether he harboured the silent suspicion that I had been diverted by flattery. When word arrived that our program had been accepted, there was complete silence from all quarters.

Chapter Four
Stochastic Serendipity

Although our survival in New Brunswick had the wished for effect on the marketplace, nothing was ever said about our adventure, even after our programs passed muster in the main provinces we served. The same hand-wringing over the same ominous fears occupied the industry chatter, whether it came from the IBC or from the nerve centers in our branches. The invariable responses amounted to the standard, hopelessly minimal pulse-taking, a process called calculating the ELR, or earned loss ratio, followed in short order by head-shaking admissions that it didn't prove anything because the numbers concealed an indeterminate number of counter-balancing forces. Nowhere was there a mechanism that could be tapped for samples of the requisite information to pinpoint a cause or verify an intuition, much less one that routinely gathered relevant data with a frequency adequate to monitor a developing trend. Worse yet was the sense of being

Token Woman: The One That Got Away

directionless; no one had any plan, not even an expressed desire to conjure one.

With no ghost of experimenting-past, present or future apparent in the chiefs' consciousnesses, where was the authorization, or even recognition, of Merlin-esque projects to come from; it seemed clear to me that the misfortunes of the industry were due to faulty leadership in significant places. Still, the possibility existed that somewhere in the hierarchy, there was a chief who not only had the wisdom to envision new possibilities but also the will to risk trying them. At least there had to be a best candidate, though my inventory of possibilities did not look promising.

The first candidate to consider was my mentor. If he still harboured any illwill over the New Brunswick affair, he never raised it but there was no collegiality either. When his day had gone well at the IBC, he became a genial but decidedly stuffy old chap. Our communication otherwise was awkward. As a chief, I became convinced that he made a better Watson than Holmes. His agenda for me consisted of more legions of numbers marching off a borrowed teletype. His plan, if it could be so called, was clearly not pro-active. He seemed content for me to now sit and wait until someone, as yet unknown, pronounced the ratemaking exercise a success or failure. How or when this would be determined did not concern him, though he openly acknowledged that there were fundamental weaknesses in the chiefs' expectations for the custom ratemaking scheme.

The flaw in the scheme was the distinct possibility that market realities, combined with the poorly-founded classification scheme, would render the custom rate structure plan futile, the equivalent of attempting to nail jelly to the wall. For example, since the age of the driver actually was only statistically related to the quality of the risk, the act of raising the rates for some whole age-class to a different extent than our competitors would tend to encourage more of the better drivers in that class to seek insurers who rewarded accident-free history or lower mileage or some other loophole in the classification scheme. The resulting mix of our policyholders in that age-class would then shift unpredictably, invalidating the statistical basis for the rate. Conversely, lowering the rates for some class would bring in more policyholders in that class, conceivably altering the quality of the group's risk.

Whether this would happen, or was happening, whether there was a better classification scheme, would be determined elsewhere; academia possibly, though they were out of touch with real world data, or in smoke-filled back room negotiations where the doability would be traded for industry-wide acceptability and political desirability to major players. My originally vague dissatisfaction with the lack of substance in the classification scheme had been set aside while I focussed

Token Woman: The One That Got Away

on the essentials of producing the structure and learning the ropes. Now though, the inherent flaws seemed to cry for examination; but fatalism or risk-aversion or other priorities yielded a colorless horizon.

Next on my list of candidates were the chiefs committed to the shareholders' laws. Their highest vision was a policy management system linking our branch underwriting functions with accounting and claims, incorporating our current paperhandling and forms and reports. Though admirable and desirable, it was strictly the usual tank-operation. It was designed to mimic the existing world but with better communication to accommodate the intended growth of the company. There was no capability built-in to do ratemaking, statistical enquiry, simulations or any of the other wizardry I was looking for. Interlopers with intentions of any such wild unruliness would not be tolerated. Such tampering was not only incompatible, it was an unholy infringement on their territory and treasure.

Nor was there any hope from the Society of winged beasts. The Society was home to both species of winged beast, life and non, and their program for non-life winged beasts was a less than satisfactory adaptation that barely acknowledged the property and casualty actuary's different world. Unfortunately. it was my only official guidance in actuarial matters and its sum total consisted of a list of exams, each with a preparatory textbook. I found myself immersed in the study of Life Contingencies, an interesting but irrelevant tour of the many-faceted formulas needed to estimate premiums for every conceivable life insurance, pension and annuity form. Had that been an isolated detour in a program devoted to wizardry, the incentive of future wonders might have alleviated my impatience. But the later texts looked even worse; more relevant, yes, but dry, non-mathematical catalogs of policy forms and legal technicalities. Not a shred of evidence to support the future I was seeking; and the only sign of change in Society programming was news of an argument among the board members over the use of calculators in the math examinations. Calculators! A tool that had already proved itself useless in the real world of ratemaking, a major part of actuarial science. My mentor could see some use, some confirmation of worth, in this news, for my discarded programmable calculator, but I was less than impressed with this so called innovation.

    The incongruity between the Society's program and my expectations suggested that my original vision in the library of Merlin-esque adventures had been a trip to the Twilight Zone. Yet my daily exposure to our problems showed exactly the type of needs the brochure had described. Somewhere in the ranks of winged beasts there were advocates of the wizardry we needed but they weren't accessible to me. For a while I continued working my way through the Society's exercises but my time

Token Woman: The One That Got Away

was too scarce and too precious for this useless extravagance and I fell sick of their program's content because it bore no resemblance to the quest that had summoned me from the pages of their own brochure.

While wandering in these doldrums, convinced that the key to escaping this morass was to find the right chief to make use of my skills, I began considering how wide I might have to cast my net in order to find the requisite vision and determination; going outside was unpalatable but how much more searching of the ranks in-house would be productive or even conceivable.

One day after most of the tribes had gone in search of lunch, I was winding down some lengthy calculation when the peace and quiet was unaccountably breached by a weary, exasperated voice leaping over my partition. Not only was the sound startling but the content was astounding. 'Stochastic, what is stochastic! Why can't they at least use words that are in the dictionary!' Somehow, the gravitational pull of new ideas had brought my path to cross with someone struggling with exactly one of the magic words in my past; it had to be a clue in my quest! With delight I answered that shockingly brash interruption with its unthinkably, improbable gift by shouting back through the shattered stillness, with equal lack of propriety, that he should interpret the magic word as random or statistical.

Stochastic Serendipity

Leaving my desk and poking around corners of other partitions til I found him, I could barely contain my curiosity. The mystery someone was KGH, the casualty underwriting chief; one of the younger chiefs, he was small of build, lean and wiry, just beginning to gray, with that air of both tension and mirth that marks quick wits. The document with the offending word he said was part of some materials sent from our London Home Office to bewilder the provincials. London had offered a workshop on cutting edge concepts to introduce new thought processes to key personnel throughout their worldwide organization. Being apparently the acknowledged whizkid of our underwriting chiefs, he had been asked by the senior chiefs to tackle this latest challenge from London.

Whether or not our senior chiefs considered this challenge to be just another volley to be lobbed back over the ocean as cleanly as we could before getting back to real business, he could visualize the relevance of these concepts particularly for a senior chief. Watching him fit various constructs to hypothetical situations from our daily existence I recognized that his aptitude for understanding mathematical concepts was much greater than he, mostly because of his myopic past school teachers, gave himself credit for. Here was not just a quick wit with an appetite for challenge; here were the aspirations, both intellectual and personal, that I was seeking; and filling his stochastic needs would become my growing intrigue.

Token Woman: The One That Got Away

Whenever there was time available, I would wander over to explore whatever new ideas he'd encountered or to offer help with whatever he was working on. Whenever he had a question, I made time available. As we worked together it became apparent that his skills complemented mine. More than that, there was that collegiality, that compatibility of temperament and acceptance of differences that made communication easy; and so a camaraderie developed in which we could almost anticipate each other's moves. None of this seemed to concern my mentor since I made sure my tasks were done at end of day.

The day eventually came when there were changes in our marching orders. Death had recently claimed our most senior chief in Canada and the powers in London had installed an unknown transplant from New Zealand whose connections there made him a relative of the twelve month tribe. After a suitable period the new senior chief was ready and the new marching order began to take shape. KGH was a major beneficiary. The speed, the mobility, the lack of fanfare, all suggested more of a coup than a promotion.

KGH had moved to his new office and he called me in for a closed door discussion. He had arranged for me to report to him but he was hastening to reassure me that his view of our relationship was much more that of colleagues. In his words he proposed that I would be his 'office wife' which, to him, meant that although the outside world of rules and conventions would see him as head of our team, within our operating world I would be his co-equal. His unfortunate choice of phrasing was somewhat alarming considering the dark struggles I was experiencing on the homefront; those conflicts were very carefully contained so no one would ever guess because Yitz was as persuasive an advocate of women's liberation then as when we had first met. But KGH's temperament was much more restrained and civil, making his proposal more an unintended mockery of my earlier indiscretions than a hint of anything to come. Besides the quest that he was offering was the one for which I had come, the one I had prepared for so carefully in long years of mental discipline; and those prospects so excited me, reviving visions of Camelot in my daytime dreams, that I envied his wife's liberation and marveled at the wealth the senior chiefs had allocated for our adventure.

They had blessed our union with new titles, new structures, new playmates and a new toy. KGH was now the Vice President of Underwriting and I was, officially, the company Statistician. The toy was an IBM 5110, an early mini computer, that was to be mine for testing. It came with some experimental software and the limited services of two consultants from the States to the South. Although the playmates and toys were likely a concession to the powers in London and were planned to be only temporary, there was a

Token Woman: The One That Got Away

theoretical chance that the senior chiefs might be persuaded to keep them permanently.

All of this raised the eyebrows of the other chiefs, mostly because my former mentor had more seniority, more industry stature. Not only had he been passed over for VP of Underwriting but his department had disappeared and I had surfaced in the court of the apparent victor. The official reason was his health; he had heart trouble and continued to avidly smoke his elegant pipe; and the senior chiefs had explained that not only was the VP position very stressful for its occupant but, even if he were willing to take the risk, the company had just experienced the turmoil that death could cause in the ranks of senior chiefs. His new position was very ambassadorial; he was our official Industry Representative; his portfolio was to expand our role and protect our interests in the political processes that were making the rules for the industry's facility pool for uninsurable drivers because participation in this necessary evil was a delicate, public matter.

Into this turmoil among the ranks, the senior chiefs dropped the other shoe. Right out from under the noses of our competitors and co-subscribers to the industry clearinghouse, the senior chiefs had managed to lure the only Canadian winged beast, Veljo Taht, from his lair at the IBC! To most of the chiefs this was reassuring, clearly demonstrating the company's appeal to a prized new chief and confirming their own prestige as a member of that company. To others, the rumoured size of his inducement undermined the points scored for prize acquisition. To a very few, there was some concern that this maneuver might generate illwill among our competitors, making political cohesion awkward, at least for a time. Much could depend on the impact of the winged beast, himself.

The bearded wonder, complete with his own tribe, was to take up residence on the far side of the office, beyond the investment tribe. He was bringing with him his assistant at the IBC who had recently achieved the status of associate winged beast, thereby completely depleting the IBC's pool, and another, more junior staffer. They were to report directly to the senior chiefs, giving the winged beast maximum liberty and access. But there was more comment among the chiefs about this new tribe's trademark, their hirsute faces, a characteristic totally unknown in the industry.

On paper as well as geographically, it appeared that our paths would not often cross with the winged beast and his tribe, since our explicit mission was to explore the esoteric techniques being promoted from abroad. But our territories were not so separable, at least not from the vantage point of my vision in the library. In my view, if our efforts to establish Merlin-esque ideas failed to breach the main actuarial territories, then the power of this magic would never be

Token Woman: The One That Got Away

realized. Applying its force to molehills when there were mountains that needed moving would waste its brilliance, fail to solve the critical problems of our industry and leave the impression of irrelevance and expendability. We would remain, at best, a shaky affair of a remote and minor province.

Geographically, our province was located in the cubicles near the claims and underwriting tribes in an area reclaimed from a few clericals. The tribe was to consist of Mary who was KGH's secretary, and Nermin whom we were adopting from the accounting tribe. As I began exploring the capabilities of our new toy, I initiated them to the wonders it could perform and we shared many conversations and visions. These quiet enthusiasms and our informal bonds of days gone by became our routine of march, without benefit or burden of official hierarchy.

Chapter Five
Decision Trees

Our new playmates called themselves Decision Support consultants and arrived with their 5110 software to acquaint us with its features. Their offices were in Washington DC in the States to the South; and their usual clients were Pentagon Chiefs. Apparently those chiefs now had fewer puzzles to entertain our consultants because the Vietnam War was history, and so our itinerant wizards had planned to branch out into the corporate marketplace. Their firm had put together a version of the military's decision analysis software attempting to scale it down to run on IBM's new mini. Eager to be among the first beneficiaries of the military, we had agreed to beta-test this mini-computer version of their software and to report to our chiefs on the viability of these techniques in the real world of our insurance environment.

That we were leaving the 'real' world was not just the opinion of the conservatives among our chiefs. Realizing that

Token Woman: The One That Got Away

our playmates, though experts in the psychology of decision making, had no prior exposure to the world of insurance and that, in any event, they would not be readily available once our brief intro was concluded, made our situation less than reassuring. To complete this recipe for a wilderness adventure was the added feature that both hardware and software were experimental. Our mini was the only one of its kind in Canada at that point, so support was unlikely and maintenance, if needed, would be a nightmare. As piece de résistance, the software was a beta version; not even a dreaded one-point-oh would likely have as many surprises.

The program performed exactly one function; it 'rolled up' decision trees. Now this was not a small task. These entities, these decision trees, were graphic representations of all the possible outcomes of the decision being analyzed, including all the values and likelihoods attached to each event-path leading from the decision to an outcome. 'Rolling up' meant calculating a summary value for each available choice, taking into account all the events, likelihoods, and outcome values branching from that choice and indicating the worth, the expected value, of that choice. By comparing these expected values, the one making the decision could see which choice held the greatest expected benefit; or if none of them was favorable then the choice that held the least expected cost.

The problem for the program was that these trees could be very bushy, and worse, their shape could be so very different from one decision to the next that no constraints could be assumed by the programmer, making a substantial amount of data preparation necessary. The decision maker needed to identify each available option and trace all of its consequences to their eventual resolution. The only available way to keep track of all the data was to chart the whole tree. Manually sketching those branches, for realistic scenarios, was an extended process that typically required drawing paper the size of horse blankets.

   After the complete tree was drawn, came the valuation phase of this data preparation. At each point where the future could branch, someone had to gauge the likelihood of each branch, assigning each of those branches an appropriate probability. Since the branches, which emanated from any one of these 'event nodes', collectively had to describe the entire range of possibilities at that point, the probabilities assigned to the branches at an event node had to add to 100%; another thing to be confirmed. When the complete array of branches had been drawn out and the probabilities assigned to each branch, the decision maker then had to gauge the benefit or cost of arriving at the endpoint of each possible sequence of branches. Even using hypothetical problems, this assigning of benefits or costs to each endpoint was a lengthy process.

Token Woman: The One That Got Away

Finally it was time to fire up the program on our experimental behemoth and begin the correspondingly lengthy and intensely precise data input phase. But there was an immediate improvement over the teletype; our new toy had a monitor and this delightful little thing called a cursor which could be backed up, at least within the input line, til it was positioned for correcting the inevitable typographical errors. These editing features were several orders of magnitude better than peering down into the depths of the teletype, attempting the hopelessly futile process of counting 'deletes' as the unidirectional teletype carriage marched counterintuitively forward. That little cursor alone made this phase a comparative joy even while our crew hovered nervously waiting for the first sign of a dreaded 'bug'.

Although this computer was the state of the art, having as much internal memory as the mainframe that had devoured my punched cards just a few short years earlier, the complexity of the program needed to accommodate any possible tree that the decision maker could concoct made the little mini struggle. We would set it chewing on our branch relationships and probabilities while we went to lunch in the hopes that it would be nearly finished when we returned, provided we hadn't entered a tree that was too bushy and caused the machine to run out of memory. The resulting crash was terminal; it meant trimming the bush and starting again. Power it was;

Decision Trees

Star Trek it wasn't.

If our valiant little machine succeeded, it was cause for celebration, at least until we gained enough familiarity to guess what its limits were. Our toy had been dubbed 'rubber ducky' when it arrived because the chiefs, seeing for the first time a genuine mini-computer, were stunned that it occupied so much less space than the monster planned for the twelvemonth tribes' tank operation. About the size of a credenza but with a smaller footprint, our new toy came complete with its own supply of tape cartridges and IBM manuals.

Our research mandate required that we concoct, scavenge, and resurrect examples of company decisions, and then evaluate the applicability, usefulness and doability of putting them through the program's rigors in the 'real' world. Theoretically our decision makers were intuitively attempting the mental gymnastics involved in this program, calling it their gut-feel. But the more complex the decision, the more diverse the sources of information needed, the more controversial the choices, or the more levels of approval required, the less satisfactory was the old way. The cost of our new way was the discipline and its manageability.

To achieve this mandate we were expected to put this program through its paces repeatedly, evaluating time, energy, accuracy and difficulties. Our own plan was not so limited and I had requested the manuals for the language spoken by our

Token Woman: The One That Got Away

borrowed mini. The sight of its programs made most viewers cringe; APL was a heavily mathematical language; no words, just reams of formulaic constructions, matrix algebra, occasional character strings and lots of Greek letters and invented Runic symbols; and it read from right to left. A language only a mathematician could love. Love it I would need to, because, for this venture, wizardry was essential and I was on my own.

KGH had been made public leader of the underwriting chiefs and was determined to take those reins. Outwardly all was calm, even cordial, but the atmosphere had changed; space itself had become viscous, or more precisely, moving among the tribe felt vaguely, invisibly repellent, as if two poles of like magnetic charge were being brought too close together. To establish his leadership among former peers would not happen without sustained effort. His remaining on top of those restive affairs threw the load of our unauthorized expeditions upon myself as our only chance of victory. The key to our scheme was our campaign for a mini of our own. Without that assured computing power, there would be no contest. The mini had to provide the base for our long term operations.

Our official expeditions into decision trees for the company were well enough received, based on the feedback from KGH's presentations to his chiefs; but it was clear that the frequency of appropriate cases justifying the rigors of this analysis was a weakness in our campaign to keep the mini, simply for decision analysis. There was also the problem of strangeness; every chief had his own familiar report formats, ones that his eyes were trained to read and digest at a glance. The sense of being lost when facing this new output made the senior chiefs impatient, unable to focus and absorb its usage, like a race car driver reluctant to attempt being his own chief mechanic. To accommodate his chiefs, KGH manually restructured the output for his presentations; even though it seemed to me that this would perpetuate the problem into the long term.

More difficult to deal with was a different discomfort. They seemed embarrassed to see so plainly the extent to which major decisions made use of gut-feel values, as if these values contaminated the computerized surgery being performed. KGH took to repeating the list of reasons for adopting the new process, for laying it out plainly, with all the fervor of an om, a ritual, a benediction, an exorcism. Our expeditions showed them examples where counterintuitive results were justifiable based on the input assumptions as well as examples where intuitive results were sensitive to modifications of some assumptions and insensitive to modifications of other assumptions until they saw the value of accuracy and information depended on the structure of the decision. Discovering these dependencies would allow them to focus on things that mattered without diminishing or exaggerating the

Token Woman: The One That Got Away

value of gut-feel. It was just another source of information that could be examined and handled with clarity and precision.

But mostly we were caught in a conundrum; the optimal presentation scene was casual and peaceful but to appreciate the power of the technique, a rock and a hard place were what was really needed. With no immediate crisis to give need its urgency, a decision tree seemed so academic. There had to be more, much more to induce the senior chiefs to keep our rubber ducky. I needed to make this toy indispensable, to build bridges to the many points along their daily routes, to seamlessly integrate the unreal nuts and bolts of early mathematical computing into the 'real world' of a senior chief, without ruffling any more eyebrows.

Chapter Six
Twelve Month Moving Premonitions

Before we could make our mini indispensable, we discovered that there were preliminary hurdles we had to cross, because the sight of simple things like routine hardware and software maintenance sent the natives scattering like nervous sparrows. It was as if feeding a cartridge into the machine might expose them to something contagious, obscene or at least uncouth. To our relief, they were not overtly hostile; they had no trouble at all in referring to it as rubber ducky, but in a tone that revealed more jitters than pure disparagement. It was more a case of being afraid to be curious. Their avoidance did not extend to making the computer's presence unspeakable. In fact, they almost vied for the opportunity to make a clever remark about our little beast. This would be the hook we needed to draw them in. We needed to be quick, to get the game afoot, to keep the ball in play. Before the novelty wore off, we had laid a threefold plan of marketing, service and

Token Woman: The One That Got Away

entertainment.

Our marketing objective was straightforward; create a positive aura that would induce the natives to consider our overtures. At the very least, it was important to keep the tribes engaged so they could not ignore our feats, diminishing them into insignificance, virtual oblivion. With the power to solve so many of their dilemmas it seemed so frustrating that we should need a campaign to overcome their reluctance. We responded warmly to any comer but our main tactic was to repeat the successful stir created by our mini's accidental naming. Carefully, I christened each of our ventures to invite their curiosity, to amuse and provoke delight, to calm their tribal jitters, to stay always in their mind's eye.

The actuarial staff, by contrast, withdrew into their officially defined spaces, aloof on good days and arrogant on bad ones. It was not uncommon to hear a phone slammed down, to meet a glowering countenance. There was no measuring the bad grace of the trainee actuaries or their chief, none of whom was ever seen to consult or mingle. This clearly helped us now and again but it made it difficult to properly gauge their strength.

My unofficial staff's natural sensitivity to the tribe's feelings and our eagerness to ease the chiefs' discomfort, to gain their trust, was a matter of considerable pride among us. These skills were so undervalued in the market and their value so apparent to us that we may have over-valued them, but only in the same proportion as we felt would compensate for the market's injustice. This part of our strategy clearly aided our marketing effort but it made it impossible not to despise our adversaries for their deficiency, an unhealthy attitude that has frequently been a serious source of strategic error in campaigns, and will certainly be again.

But for the moment, their bad grace might be made use of, and so we undertook an extensive plan of entertainment, at least as grand as our limited resources allowed. At first we borrowed the personnel tribe's remote little conference room with simple accommodations; later, when the chiefs were more comfortable, we held them in actual proximity to our beast. Only when they were acclimated to its presence, did we use our mini to improve our demonstrations.

Our goal was to convince the tribes that our objective was nearer to education, which was consistent with our official mandate, as well as being imperative for the success of our unofficial goals. KGH gathered our semi-captive audience from the tribe of his underwriters with gracious invitations that frequently included charming luncheons. To complete the welcoming ambiance, we also opened these pleasant sessions to the curious of other tribes, whenever the opportunity presented. KGH used his natural gifts as host and emcee to introduce each of our casual little show-and-tells, keeping the intensity of our

Token Woman: The One That Got Away

need for converts well concealed, emphasizing instead the aura of generosity and feasting, wealth and promise.

Before these select audiences, we unveiled each of our new services, each one a gift, each one extending the reach of the third tine of our threefold plan. The demonstration of their functions, the illustration of their workings, was my part of our wooing, for a chief needs to achieve a degree of comprehension, a sense of control. Polishing their essence to emphasize the grace and art of these new concepts, we danced through the mathematics, freeing each idea from the pain of its birth. This natural ease, a new experience to the tribes, whetted their appetites and began to wear away their skepticism.

Our first objective for the service segment of our strategy was a gift for planning. Not truly a function of any single tribe, planning was the responsibility of one native in particular who was to consolidate the plans devised by each of the tribal chiefs, regardless of the calendar and mindset of his tribe. Not only was the task of securing timely cooperation for his information requests a substantial obstacle, but, like the ratemaking effort of my initiation to the insurance world, the consolidation process was prone to transcription errors, computation errors, and worst of all, the arrival at the bottom line with an unacceptable message for the senior chiefs. The potential for embarrassment in having any of the former two exposed gave our lonely planner a more harried look in planning season and may have contributed to his seriously receding hairline. But the latter difficulty in his work was the vulnerability I recognized.

Sympathy for his plight each time he had to start from scratch was a natural reaction but the familiarity of his pain was the key to my understanding. It seemed to me that the skepticism of our chiefs was vulnerable to pressure in that area for the work was repetitive to the point of being mind numbing and their relief would surely generate undeniable gratitude. To sweeten the prize was the realization that the planners came from the upper ranks of each tribe so, if we converted them to our side for this process, we would gain doubly. Not only would we benefit from their satisfaction as clients but we would gain access to their finest sources of intelligence. So in my expeditions round underwriting and claims, accounting and investments, I used planning's needs as my ticket and workload reduction as their incentive to grant me access to their best documents and resources.

Not every project was as much of an unqualified success. One of our early ventures was somewhat controversial. Though it could have been a disaster, in the end, after taking a curious twist, the payoff turned out somewhat more positive. Celebrating the chiefs' gratitude as well as the wealth of their insights, I began work on a risky bridge between the tribes. The need seemed urgent, worth the gamble and the difficulty. The

Token Woman: The One That Got Away

goal was to weave together the many layers of premium year results from the far-sighted tribes' data to produce a projection of the other tribes' precious year-end. But to be of use to the chiefs in dealing with daily news from the marketplace, the data had to reflect the most recent results, however crude.

Since premium-year data was reported only annually, I needed to find an approximation that was available more frequently. The closest choice for my basis was the accident-year data that I had encountered on my forays into claims and accounting. Claims were reported monthly but were categorized by accident-year, which, with some calculating sleight of hand, could be used as a surrogate for the claims component of premium-year data. The trick was to replace the written premiums that accounting recorded with a construction called earned premium which would then serve as the corresponding

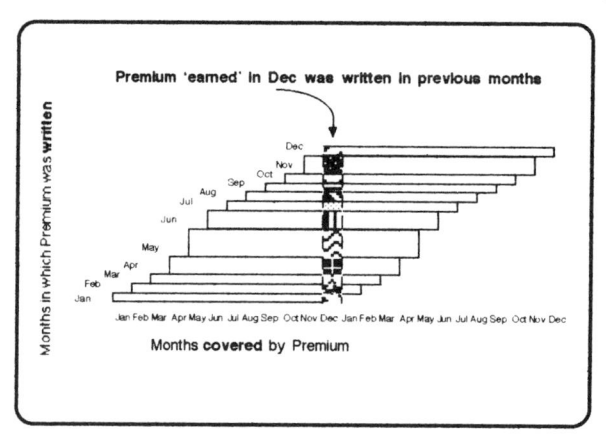

Twelve Month Moving Premonitions

surrogate for our needed 'accident-year premium'. Earning a month's premium was a straightforward process of allocating the total premium written over the previous twelve months into monthly segments and then tallying the segments that belonged to the current month. This amount gave an estimate of the risks to be covered in that month. It measured our exposure and should have been comparable to the accidents occurring over that time period if the premiums in force were adequate for their intended risks.

Where the planning project had been fundamental number-crunching, this bridge was a high-tech statistical construction that gambled on the limited histories we had gleaned from accounting as well as assumptions about appropriate curves to fit them. The histories of accident year data had one more drawback; they were recorded in year-to-date form. Since this form was extremely unstable for the first few months of the year, it was not only potentially deceptive during those early months but it also made it difficult for the chiefs to use this form as a basis for any corrective action until much of their maneuvering time before year-end was gone. Though it suited the chiefs in accounting, it was less than satisfactory for the decision needs of senior chiefs. For those decision purposes, which it was our intention to support, we chose to calculate a more appropriate form called twelve-month-moving data, simply a rolling year's worth of the

Token Woman: The One That Got Away

amounts being reported. As the months went by, this data moved more smoothly toward the eventual year-end point, at which time the twelve-month tribe's customary year-to-date number coincided with our twelve-month-moving one. To anticipate what that precious number would be, even quite early in the year, would warm the little hearts of our twelve-month tribes and especially their chiefs.

Using these twelve-month-moving histories, certain reasonable assumptions about the shapes of the curves representing each different age-layer of claims, and regression analysis to approximate those curves, rubber ducky and I arrived at an estimate. The risks, that I saw as a mathematician, were several, all related to the shortage of data and making my intended bridge not as well tested as I'd have liked. Interpreting these statistical goodness-of-fit measures was not easy even when the data was simple and well-behaved, which business data never is. But my premonitions of difficulty in using and explaining this system did not anticipate my intended audience's philosophical concerns of determinism.

While I was caught between wanting acceptance for the value of my art and wanting honest art, they were caught between wanting to know and not wanting to lose their claim to potency. At the unveiling of our Premonitions, I had braced for a barrage of questions about reliability, confidence intervals,

Twelve Month Moving Premonitions

and my logic in the choice of curves to fit, but the chiefs were alert to a far different challenge, one I had inadvertently laid at their doorstep. I had barely arrived at the end of my exposition when I sensed a certain tension in the group. They couldn't wait to see what the system said about their individual piece of the year-end, or so it seemed, yet the increased volume of chatter lacked the warmth I'd expected.

Morrison, claims chief, always keen in scenting a dilemma and delighting in angling for whatever advantage he could stir loose, put the test to me. Was I saying that this magic number for the year-end was now decided, that there was nothing he could do to change it? This was clearly the opposite of what I was trying to enable them to do and I could almost anticipate the challenge he was about to level; that he most certainly had more tricks up his sleeve than my system could imagine. Me, who was still so green and inexperienced in the fine points of managing his tribe and their resources. Not that he was at all belligerent. In fact he was the picture of mirth and innocence, except for the intensity of his delivery. Somehow I managed to recover in the nick of time and, out of the blue, came the image of a car, driving to my rescue.

As I explained that no, it was more like having the computer point out where your car will be in a short while if you keep on going at the rate and in the direction that you are driving it; and in fact the purpose of Premonitions was to give

Token Woman: The One That Got Away

our chiefs advance warning so that remedial action could be formulated if necessary. That's when I realized that not only had I found the key to his acceptance, but that solving his dilemma had provided me the escape valve I needed for the technical risks in forecasting. In the end, it didn't seem to matter whether the forecasts were accurate since they were never used. Nor did I ever recommend them later because the width and significance of the confidence intervals that the system was producing were not satisfactory for forecasting. Whenever one the chiefs referred to Premonitions, it was only the summary reports of the base data, not the forecasts, that they found desirable. Apparently, the chiefs had developed their own magical ways of using rubber ducky's Premonitions for monitoring their segments of the business. More important for our plans was the fact that I had gained Morrison as an ally. His admiration for an adversary who neatly slipped from the snares he relished, brought our little group a widening door to claims and favorable opinion among a major tribe.

Chapter Seven
Claims and Risk

Many of our forays into claims' territory were inspired by the needs of the underwriting tribe. The local members of the tribe were the company's best experts, which made them the logical destination for major underwriting projects, as well as for their branch brethren's requests for assistance. As a result, some of the most exotic casualty risks imaginable would cross their desks and they would frequently, eventually, come to us to help quantify these risks; for the local underwriting chiefs were beginning to realize that we had the skills and interest to work with them and make their brain-bogglers more bearable.

These puzzles were so intriguing because there weren't any ready made samples of data to tap. This made it imperative that we learn to value our underwriter's intuitive functioning and make our techniques practical, to meet their need for responses that were as quick as they were painfree.

Token Woman: The One That Got Away

Although we studied the distributions which we acquired from the claims tribe for the appropriate general class of risks, it was our task to elicit from the underwriter his feel for the individual risk. By carefully selecting points along the range of possible losses, we'd extract the changes in curvature that would describe the shape of the risk in graphical terms, from which we could then compute the expected loss that was implicit in his feelings.

The most curious discovery about the distributions of claims by size was their absence of normalcy. Even in the general class distributions, the bulk of the claims were so skewed toward the low end that when we graphed them for analysis, the image that emerged looked more like a ski slope than anything that could be thought of as a bell, however lopsided.

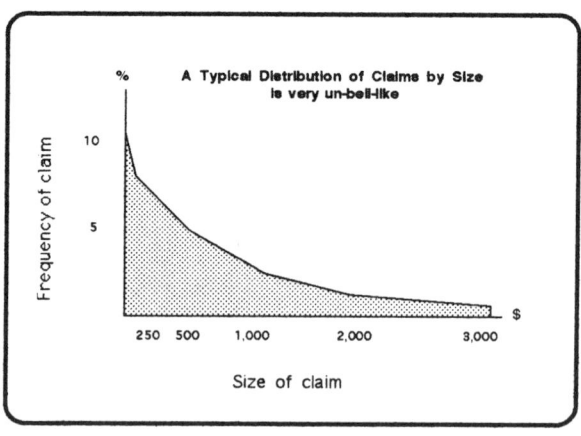

A Typical Distribution of Claims by Size is very un-bell-like

But it would be misleading to overemphasize this end of the graph because, for casualty and personal liability risks, it was the tail that wagged the dog. For these general categories, and usually more so for the exotic ones described by the chiefs, the extreme catastrophes that haunted the high end of the scale of risk were so large that they overbalanced the seemingly minuscule probabilities of their occurrence. This surprising instability made the accurate measurement of the high-end tails of these strange shapes a critical stage of our task.

Another typical underwriting project that would justify incursions into claims' territory were the situations in which the request was for unique limits or unusual deductibles. When our branch underwriters needed to tailor coverage to improve the attractiveness of our proposal in a bidding process, they would offer the potential insured various options to reduce our premium. The option of selecting higher deductibles was appealing to clients and their agents in certain situations. Although this put more responsibility on their client to cover part of the risk themselves, many larger commercial risks were quite capable of being more self-insuring. For the smaller, independent business operators these arrangements enabled them to afford coverage for the larger risks that would have bankrupted them. Using an appropriate distribution, custom or general, depending on the coverage being sought, our task was to

Token Woman: The One That Got Away

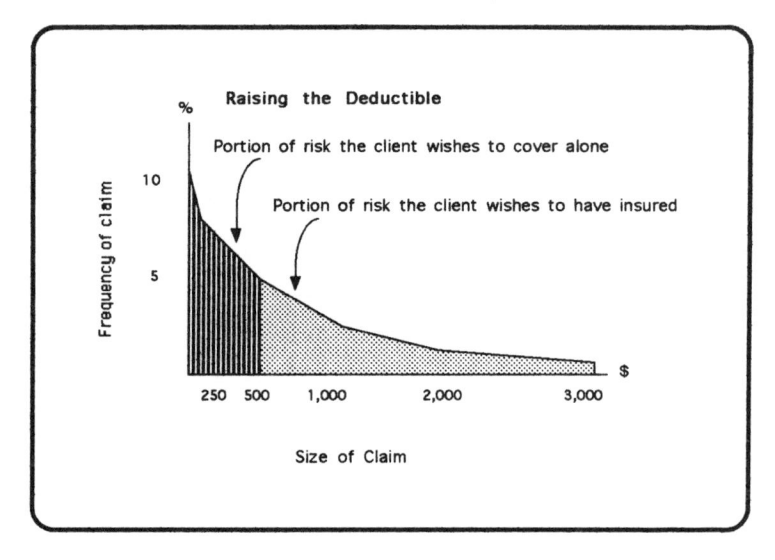

estimate the size of the distribution's segment at the low-end.

```
                    Raising the Deductible
                    Portion of risk the client wishes to cover alone
                         Portion of risk the client wishes to have insured
```

Figure: Frequency of claim (%) vs Size of Claim ($), with markers at 250, 500, 1,000, 2,000, 3,000 and frequency values 5 and 10.

Though the concept was to measure the area under the distribution curve, the technique itself was more an application of common sense and approximation theory than calculus, because the curves were not any standard function for which there were standard answers.

The unique limits requests would arise in more complex situations and focussed on the catastrophe end of the risk potential. For the really mammoth contracts, where even we would not like to have to pick up the insured's pieces by ourselves, our underwriters needed to negotiate with interested re-insurers. These companies would accept some share of the high-end risks of large contracts as well as generally offering to insure an insurance company itself, thereby spreading the risks across many companies' resources. Estimating the area under the high-end of the claims distribution, the infamous tail, enabled our underwriters to structure and evaluate offers with a greater degree of confidence.

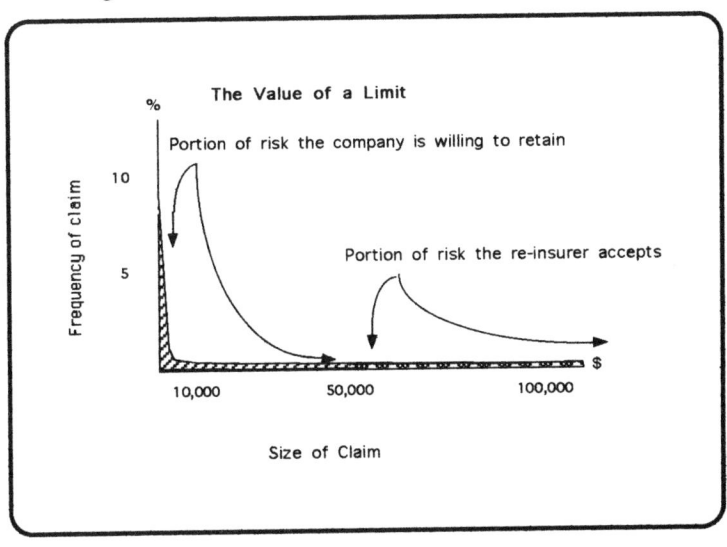

The Value of a Limit

Frequency of claim (%) vs. Size of Claim ($)

- Portion of risk the company is willing to retain
- Portion of risk the re-insurer accepts

Besides gaining insight into the functioning of both tribes, the use of their internal documents led to many concepts and measures that we could incorporate into our repertoire, making it much easier to anticipate their needs and generate reports that they could immediately understand. Instead of needing a translator, communication became more natural,

Token Woman: The One That Got Away

insider to insider, so we were able to function on a more even footing in the insurance arena. Each of our tasks was within our borders, though just barely; with KGH's encouragement, any latent resistance among my former mentor's sympathizers had apparently vaporized with the possible exception of the actuary, and we were not giving him any cause for arousing the natives.

In fact, the good press we were receiving from our clients among the chiefs was reinforcing the relations we were building with our services. On these missions, though, it was the chiefs who were entertaining. It had never occurred to me to include the company in the list of victims of a disaster so it came as a surprise to me when one of the chiefs claimed that you knew you were an insider when your first coherent thought, after the initial shock, was whether the company had a piece of this latest disaster. But after thinking about this different point of view, it seemed accurate and only natural to wonder if our tribes had been hurt or if it had been one our competitors.

Tales from the field about risks they had written seemed so exciting. Just imagining the job of evaluating risks that involved major construction projects would take my breath away. How does one even begin to imagine the casualty risks in building the CN Tower?

One of the more incredible ones was trying to estimate the potential for disaster when the blasting crews building an extension on Montreal Airport's main runway were actually expected to do their work while the big jets were still landing on it. The disaster potential, even before worrying about valuing it, was too awful to consider; how would nervous pilots be able to cope with landing there, would the tension of trying to coordinate the timing of the explosions to avoid incoming jumbos, in spite of staticky radio transmissions, affect the performance of the tower and blasting crews while they attended to their already critical functions. I wondered whether those passengers had any idea at all that they would be gliding so close above an impending explosion, whether the firefighters were lined up or just on alert. Where would an underwriter start, how would gut-feel work when the thought of the possibilities was so gut-wrenching.

It was just as amazing to see what the underwriter had used as indicators of whether the process was going to be well controlled. Running the gamut from determining the reputation of the crewleader, the blasting company's hiring practices, the financial health of the project, and the weather for that time of year, and starting from some accumulated impressions about the likelihood of more normal blasting accidents, the underwriter had arrived at the probability by some internal magic. Was it just a combination of resourceful common sense and long, keen observation of all sorts of accidents or was it just guessing; and if it was just guessing how had this industry

Token Woman: The One That Got Away

survived for centuries?

Not all the raw data they handled was so intriguing. Even part of a day looking over claim reports was more than my imagination could deal with. School bus accidents with shockingly trivial value assigned to a child's life, incidents of incredible stupidity on the part of supposed professionals, security arrangements before testifying in a fraud case involving the underworld. Nothing seemed to make the chiefs blink anymore. I didn't envy them their grasp of the concrete aspects of claims nor did the intricacies of distributions of claims by size seem to hold any appeal for these chiefs, so we had no difficulty at all with territoriality. They were appreciative and we heard many an incredible tale from the field in the process, and even learned to see catastrophe through their eyes.

The story on frequency had easily as many subplots. Of its two components, claims count and exposures, the most fundamental element of the puzzle was the exposures, the number of risks covered. The only available count data related to covered risks was policy counts and though they would not quite reflect the number of risks, such as cars or drivers, they seemed a reasonable surrogate, at least for written premium. In our Crystalball, a model conjured for planning's benefit, we simulated earned exposures as the obvious, but elegant, analog of earned premium. Among the variations we, at one time or another, found useful involved earning six-month policies separately from the annuals. The purpose of the exercise was to test whether apparent increases in frequency could simply be explained by observed shifts in the proportion of six-month policies in the company's mix of policy terms. If the increases were due to mix, then, when the mix stabilized, the claims counts should cease climbing. When the mix impact turned out to be reasonable but not definitive, we had no alternative except to continue to monitor.

These movements and simulations were sometimes complicated by seasonality, as they were in the auto insurance business we were writing in Canada. In auto there were substantial swings in volume that occurred in the spring and, to a much lesser extent, in the fall, with troughs in between. For auto, a change of mix that coincided with a seasonal peak or a change in total volume, would have been much more complicated than in other situations.

Even more intriguing were the delays. On the claims side there were the familiar reporting delays that we had encountered in ratemaking. These were expected to show the impact of prior changes in exposures and were also monitored in our Premonitions.

On the exposure side there were the processing delays. The routine variations in workload backup that occurred because of the time of year would be smoothed over by our

Token Woman: The One That Got Away

twelve-month-moving techniques. It was the uncommon changes in processing times that raised anxiety levels and warranted attention. Many were expected to occur later, when we finally began the long awaited and dreaded conversion to the new policy management system, to which the company was devoting major amounts of money and manpower. These delays also made estimating the berg from the size of its leading tip an exciting game every time some competitive move or government regulation rolled ashore.

Competitive moves usually consisted of rating changes, and since our chiefs' conservatism as well as our continuing need to include industry data in our calculations tended to make these shifts in market share relatively minor, and more gradual, at least compared to what government regulations did, the processing delays for these moves were usually insignificant. When the government intervened in our business, they could impact normal processing delays for both claims and exposures. Provincial governments sometimes mandated coverage changes or even, like they did in British Columbia, changed their mind from one election to another on whether to take over the auto insurance business or not.

What was left, after accounting for these other movements, should have been the elusive trends that everyone was so sure were about to swamp us. Although the longterm picture that emerged, with the benefit of smoothing, was not linear, the chiefs were satisfied with the short-term view of the direction of change. Frequency was not seen as a problem as long as it was not rising rapidly or did not fail to turn back down after several months, a time frame appropriately consistent with the underwriters' concerns about marketing strategies. Although the extent to which these strategies altered the quality of our business was unquantified, it was an area where the chiefs felt they had more chance of taking some control.

One of the government regulations that caused the chiefs many grey hairs was the wave that brought in our first ship. Canada's rising inflation was more severe than its citizens were willing to tolerate and so the federal government was under pressure to get that menace under control and do it quickly. In their efforts to strangle Canada's double digit inflation, the government enacted profit freezes so ill-considered no sane group could have conceived them.

With incredible unfairness, the Canadian feds dictated that every business, without exception, must freeze their profits, or their losses, at their last year's mark. Clearly they were perpetuating the economy's distortions of the worst kind; they legislated losses for the cautious who were slow in responding to the runaway inflation and they continued the exaggerated profits for those who had pumped inflation's flames with price increases in excess of the trends. Blind with fear or some dark stupidity, these feds threatened to force

Token Woman: The One That Got Away

premium refunds just as our premiums were catching up with our claims.

Not only was this unfair and not likely to be effective, but it would put a future burden on our business. If we attempted to carry out this insane directive, the fact that the amount would have to be spread over the entire list of all our policyholders was going to make the amount each insured received quite small, just a few dollars; and the expense of having to program, generate and mail all those refunds would have been majorly unpleasant. To complete the absurdity, the inadequacy of those premiums would simply cause the ratemaking formulas for the following year to produce that much higher increases for our clients. For the company, the impact was multiple; we would be saddled with an insupportable amount of work, a financial loss for another year and a possible loss of goodwill and marketshare the following year when the premiums returned to their expected levels.

Faced with this absurd situation, the chiefs could not realistically even consider following through with this insanity. That's when they realized the existence of another way to meet the legislated requirement to produce a loss without incurring the need to execute the fed's impossible demands. Not only would this approach avoid trouble, it would solve a major problem that the claims tribe had been warning was about to make our financial results unfavorable for years to come, even if our premiums reached the appropriate levels for those future years. Premonitions confirmed that the claim reserves that had been set over the last couple years were proving to be less than adequate to cover the costs now required to be paid since the inflation had seriously outrun their estimates. The chiefs looked to the claims tribe and our relationship with the claims tribe was handsomely confirmed when they turned to us for help in coping with this madness.

Morrison's ace was his reserving strategy but he needed to be sure that his adjustments, for pessimism, would retain their air of realism so we entered the actuaries' arena of claims development and reserving adequacy. I christened our model Houdini, celebrating our escape from those shackles, and captured the fancy of our chiefs with scenarios tailored to their control efforts. With a truly impressive sleight of hand, accounting for the humanity of his troops, Morrison was the hero of the hour.

Token Woman: The One That Got Away

Chapter Eight
MAU & Quantifying Unquantifiable Regrets

There were other strategies we depended on, between raids on actuarial territories. In these, we would concede to the actuaries their rights, but claim the high ground for our own, among the senior chiefs, as their representatives. The game seemed so obvious to us that we could not dream of the actuaries missing the maneuver but they were so focussed on claiming their rightful territory that they never realized that they were missing the area of real danger. Our success depended on keeping them so deceived.

The Newfoundland episode was one of these. The question rose because of our continuing losses in that province, coupled with their regulators' intransigence over rating increases. The nature of what our response to this situation should be became a controversial topic among the chiefs, with chiefs of different tribes taking diametrically opposite points of view. Some were quite aggressive in their point of view, insisting that we should withdraw our services entirely from the province and went so far as to suggest encouraging other insurers to do the same. Others were more conciliatory in approach, because such an action was not done except by smaller companies unable to withstand an extended period of losses. The branch chiefs were naturally alarmed and concerned for the welfare of their indians, not just appearances.

The actuary had taken the lead in projecting the picture of future losses. He emphasized our responsibility to our London Home Office, insisting that rate adequacy was their area of competence, reminding everyone that an actuary was required to sign official approvals, documents stating that it was their professional opinion that the rating structure was adequate. He concluded that the only sound alternative for the senior chiefs to choose was to cease writing business in the province.

This did not please the tribes that spent their days in the marketplace. They spoke passionately of intangibles such as industry leadership, branch morale and agent support. To their keen eyes, total withdrawal would make us seem to the rest of Canada like petty, robber barons. To Canadians with their more comprehensive social insurance system, the objective of insurance was to spread risk, to make risk bearable, and a large company should be able to sustain losses in one area of their business, such as auto, while their other areas were not so

Token Woman: The One That Got Away

problematic. Partial withdrawal was not much better and would leave the surviving indians in disarray, fearing for their own futures and unable to effectively counter the negative reactions of the independent agency force. The residents of Newfoundland may have been seen as strange and unconventional by their more affluent neighbors but that only made them seem more vulnerable in any confrontation with a large multinational company, making our remaining business there less viable.

Home Office in London began taking an interest and so our senior chiefs, whose sympathies lay with the market tribes, were concerned about justifying whatever direction they would choose. There were considerable dangers and arguments whichever way they looked. Clearly, they required firm, defensible ground for their stance. This was the opening for our own gambit.

We took the shaman's role to bring all views clearly and fairly to bear. KGH gathered together the chiefs from each of the tribes and arranged a group consultation in which each view was represented and explored, without any sense of animosity. The chiefs responded with an impressive display of team playing enabling them to focus on the problem instead of positions. To see the whole picture we needed to combine the intangible aspects of the problem with the already quantified loss picture. KGH proposed using an approach in which each aspect of the problem was assigned its own share of the total significance of the eventual outcome, resolving the issue of keeping each aspect in perspective. For each of these aspects, we then quantified the chiefs' druthers, or more precisely their regrets. As we discussed each aspect, the chief with the most expertise in that area gave his considered opinion of how much the company would regret the likely result in that area if the company took a given direction. Regrets were expressed on a common numeric scale, from -100 for most regrettable in the area under consideration, to 0 for the least regrettable. Applying the value the chiefs had agreed on for the significance of the area, to the regrets for the area, we summarized all the regrets for each different choice.

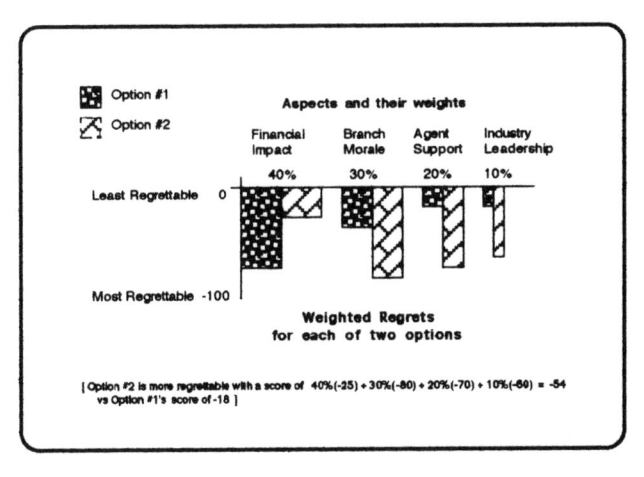

[Option #2 is more regrettable with a score of 40%(-25) + 30%(-80) + 20%(-70) + 10%(-60) = -54 vs Option #1's score of -18]

In the end the conclusion of this approach was not to

Token Woman: The One That Got Away

withdraw from the province, even though the initial impression, as we had gone round the conference room listening to the chiefs' explain their points of view, had been that the company needed to take some action putting the regulators on notice. Though this had filled our group with a sense of dread and made the final result that much more surprising, the chiefs were satisfied with the logic that produced their unexpected conclusion and especially the way it encapsulated the whole picture, giving each opinion its agreed weight. MAU, this higher wisdom whose full name was multi-attribute utility analysis, pleased our senior chiefs and mollified the powers in London, as well as unifying our local tribes for once, which doubly pleased the chiefs.

Chapter Nine
The Climate and Which Way the Wind Blew

When I arrived in this land, its population was hopelessly skewed, its few female inhabitants isolated in mind and space, as much from one another as from the ranks of chiefs. There was an invisible typing pool, located elsewhere, and a sprinkling of secretaries, floor receptionists and an occasional clerk of the female persuasion. On the floor where most of the chiefs resided, the number was barely more than a handful. Nor was commerce with one's neighbors encouraged. The sight of two women together was unknown, not counting the little group of the senior chiefs' secretaries who sat together in an open area outside the offices near the boardroom. The air was very purposeful with socializing fairly confined to the arrival of the tea wagon, mid-morning and mid-afternoon. In the beginning I was preoccupied with my new job, exploring my surroundings and its resources but after a while I began to feel that there was something missing.

Token Woman: The One That Got Away

Remembering that when I had been teaching at SUNY in Brockport, my closest associates had been women who had the same interests, my horizon now seemed more empty until I finally discovered two other young mothers whose ideas coincided with my current passions, not all of them pleasant. Our first and greatest loss was the absence of our children. Every day when we left for work, the same pain of leaving our precious little ones was there to remind us of the sacrifice we hoped would ultimately make their futures better. That pain was a unifying force that drew our group together.

Sharing our worries over unsatisfactory daycare, ways to keep our children's spirits up, coping with their many needs, reinforced our own shattered resolve. The fear that someday we would wake up to find that we had no acceptable care for our children was one that we all dreaded facing. One day when I encountered that petrifying dilemma, I decided to do the unthinkable. The day I brought Michael to the office made nervous history among the chiefs.

When Michael was even younger and I was teaching on a local campus, there were times I had brought him to tutorial sessions. He was a child, and not a doll, but he had behaved so admirably. Now that he was older I felt he could comfortably cope with the environment at my office if he were simply adequately prepared. Dressed in his best suit, he sat reading his supply of books, drawing, and exploring the recesses of my

The Climate & Which Way The Wind Blew

desk. Only once did he need a little extra attention. The office that day was more quiet than usual, as if the chiefs were holding their breaths, collectively wondering what other strangenesses were imminent. Feeling that my child was apparently unwelcome, I decided that we would not be repeating our daring little experiment. Later KGH, seeming somewhat abashed, said that he would not mind if I took the day off whenever this situation arose again. I wondered if that was a warning or just a helpful alternative, since he had seemed supportive the day of Michael's historic visit. If he had been chastised and was unwilling to admit it, then there were some among the other chiefs who were still opposed to considering on-site childcare for their indians, even though the university now had it for their faculty on the main campus.

The women who were childless or single lived differently, spoke and thought differently. Even though their numbers began to increase after a couple years, the local population never grew large enough for any but a rudimentary sense of community, age being the attracting factor; a few older, prim executive secretaries, a few younger, single clerks, and our cluster of young mothers. In our atomic separateness we shared our schemes of coping and dreams of how we'd change the world to have our children with us, seeming to satisfy some certainty that endured in our consciousness from ancient tribal custom. Keeping our sense of connection and support, we worked without

Token Woman: The One That Got Away

missing a beat, as industrious as any of the silent ones. Based on this intuitive sense of what we needed, we had removed the internal walls to increase our group's communication and found it beneficial. The benefits of this exchange may not have been apparent to others but it clearly helped diminish those outside distractions that young mothers need to deal with; it lifted our spirits to know that we were not alone; and the camaraderie contributed to our teamwork. Interspersed naturally with exchanges about our progress on our various departmental projects, the constant updating made artificial management practices unnecessary.

Even though the company offered many perks and other benefits, the only one that seemed more geared to our needs, than it was to the men's, was flextime. We wrung every advantage, used every angle of this one solution to our personal needs as young mothers. Among the many variations that was useful in the beginning, when Michael was just starting Montessori, was a break-of-day version. Isaac, for that's what my husband changed his name to when he finally got his own career launched, scheduled his consulting appointments for afternoon hours. Coming in before sunup, I had the majority of my work completed by the time Isaac dropped Michael at the door. Toronto had so many lovely places for Michael and I to explore before we rode the subway to his school. Museums, planetarium, conservatory. The days were very hectic and exhausting but we had such fun together. Flextime was a very advanced concept in the middle 70's and we gratefully built our lives around it, proud that we worked for a company that was breaking ground on the issues that mattered to us.

Some customs of Corporate Canada puzzled me endlessly, remaining unsolved for years. The secrecy surrounding paychecks boggled my simple mind and the rebuke for leaving my payslip lie open on my desktop was totally unexpected; after all my salary was automatically deposited so it wasn't that there was a question of security. Since it didn't seem that this reprimand was to protect me from my own carelessness, it had to be because of the fact that my salary was in plain view, where anyone passing my desk could see how much I was making. If I didn't care who knew, why did 'they'? What was the secret transgression? It was apparently too obvious or too horrible. That was when I remembered the time at SUNY when the union had made an issue of faculty salaries; but when I thought about that possibility here, there didn't seem to be any sign of activity. I discarded that idea, leaving the puzzle unsolved.

Another truly confusing signal, also from the personnel tribe, was the incident of the newsletter. When there were finally a couple women elsewhere in the company outside the ranks of typists inhabiting the invisible pool, the editor did a feature on Chercher la Femme. All quite nice, but something

Token Woman: The One That Got Away

just didn't sit right. Being the most senior among the group, I found it curious that Gerry Stafford should double the meaning of my 'statistics'. When we reviewed the photos that the personnel tribe had commissioned for the article, he had insisted on using the one that he claimed made me look friendly, even though I had expressed a preference for one that looked more impressive. Since it was his publication, I figured it should be his judgment call, but the reference to my 'vital statistics' made me wonder. That's when I noticed that the title for both the French and the English version was in French. At the time it didn't seem important, just curious, but later when I checked the French dictionary, even the title could be interpreted crudely as procuring.

    It had seemed only natural to trust Gerry, after all he was Bryan Burton's protege and Bryan, head of the personnel tribe, had been the one responsible for my hiring. Vaguely uneasy, I realized that, although it was the personnel tribe that was responsible for our opportunity and that harassment was unthinkable in the gentleman's code of our Anglo chiefs, it seemed their intended tribute revealed something unsavory beneath their attempt at humor, something that might be no different than my husband's double standard. Publicity was one of our goals but who were our allies?

    Among the more pleasant curiosities of Corporate Canada were the clubs. Each chief was awarded a membership

The Climate & Which Way The Wind Blew

in a club whose exclusivity was to mark his rank. The chiefs could use their club for all their business entertaining at the company's expense. This arrangement was very liberal but after I thought about it, it was another example of a perk that was more suited for male chiefs than for me. Although the men could talk business with their friends over lunch and charge it to the company, there were so few women at the level that would have been considered as contributing to the company's interests, that I probably would have seldom used it. In fact, some exclusive clubs were just changing their rules. The ancient, Canadian political Albany had just ruled its doors open to those of the female persuasion. But none were members, and visitors to its hallowed marble halls and its levantine private dining rooms were the intrepid few. This was KGH's club and on typical lunches with him, I felt on exhibit because I was the only woman. It didn't seem to bother KGH at all that everyone in the hall was staring at us. Even though we never planned or discussed this aspect of our lunches, when I thought about how long women had been excluded from such places, I felt that we were breaking new ground and that it was so daring being in the middle of a controversial experiment. It was such an exciting idea I decided I didn't even mind the little butterflies that went with being the center of so much silent attention.

As a junior chief, I was given a Board of Trade membership and KGH and I divided our time between clubs,

Token Woman: The One That Got Away

since lunch was our most consistent time to stay in touch with each other's part of our venture. But that wasn't all. Dining with KGH was always a delightful and charming experience as we ranged widely over all the world's intellectual territory, just as Isaac and I had done when we were first falling in love. And the excitement of accompanying KGH to his staid all-male social club made our business lunches unqualified adventures.

Back at the office, Mary and Nermin, my trusted friends, held down the fort. Mary had been a secretary when I arrived. She had worked her way clear of the pool and was determined to make a better life for herself and her children. That determination and her innate intelligence and curiosity led her to volunteer her services, and her free time, to assist me in loading the masses of history to the computer base in the days I served as winged beast. Ever eager to learn more, Mary gravitated to those areas of our projects that were a natural bridge from her office managing background. She became an expert in the mini's operating system, ran the jobs that generated our production reports, organized and managed our library of printout and media. Her skill at improvising and her knowledge of office routine and resources was invaluable. She ultimately became my data operations manager in fact, though not in name. In the beginning, the company only saw her as KGH's secretary.

As a single mother, she fought all the battles well,

The Climate & Which Way The Wind Blew

learned all the ropes and survived a disastrous marriage to a volatile, ex-Romanian freedom-fighter, who occasionally lurked in the shadows. Persistent and expert at probing, she knew from her own hard won experience the fine points of restraining orders and other domestic relations nightmares; she could steer you through the mazes of government subsidies, how to find decent living space in spite of the housing authority, who to call to deal with a Python between the walls.

Diminutive, pretty, with long dark hair and fair skin, she looked too delicate to cope with public school bureaucrats to protect sensitive Timmy and independent Donika, to deal with perpetually disappearing daycare for Beita. I counted on her fire and skill and some counted on her shoulder to cry on. She was our link to the younger, single women, patiently coaching them through the rough spots in their relationships. But with her current significant other, some days she needed a shoulder for herself. The only time I saw her really flinch was the day she and her children were viciously harassed on the subway by Jamaican women over her youngest's inter-racial otherness.

Nermin, our exotic and youngest member, had been an accounting clerk before joining our group. To earn that position she had had to hide her science degree since it was incompatible with her chances, as an immigrant, of getting a job. Joining us after the arrival of rubber ducky, KGH arranged

Token Woman: The One That Got Away

for her personnel records to be updated to keep her from being fired. With us, she became an analyst, compiling tables, annotating our rough graphing output, and later began learning the basics of coding and programming.

There was a subtle and delightful cadence in Nermin's voice that made everything she said seem musical. Both sensuous and dignified, with stunning dark brown eyes that conveyed her quiet amusement at the world's daily surprises, Nermin seemed knowing beyond her years. Some of the charm of her alertness and skepticism was undoubtedly due to the wonders she'd witnessed as a cross-cultural traveler.

In contrast to Mary's isolation in the outside world, Nermin came amply supplied with family, including parents, in-laws, and more. They were Shias of East Indian descent who had fled Tanzania, during political trouble there. Barely out of school, she had watched government officials extort unofficial fees from emigres. Although her family had succeeded in avoiding these transactions, they had had to come to Canada, almost one by one. Regrouping once they were safely free, they filled Nermin's life at home with old world ways and rules.

Fascinating vignettes emerged in Nermin's stories of family: neti pot and eastern medical rituals; ghee-rich recipes prepared with generations of maternal concern for Nermin's postpartum nutritional needs.

The Climate & Which Way The Wind Blew

More conservative, Nermin was the one that struggled with a dual cultural identity, trying to please the elders to preserve her connection to her roots but never quite succeeding because of her westernized education. The tension created in the younger generation of her family was likely the source of her own husband's inconvenient migraine headaches. But it never seemed to daunt her commitment to being liberated.

After the birth of Nermin's baby, she became more dependent on her family's sheltering connection. We almost envied this security except for one lingering doubt. Though Nermin's baby had assurances of family daycare, it pained her when her little one preferred another at end of day.

Though we worked closely throughout the day, our missions into territories not our own were never in number. The sight of women in the office was becoming more routine and our group's collaboration was being accepted but we noticed that it was somehow a different situation when we were in motion, especially outside our own area. Together on a mission, our group would be even more conspicuous among the tribes than separately and we did not want to alarm the natives.

This solitary mode of operation required, from each of us, far more intellectual initiative, persistence, enthusiasm than the female clerical hierarchies of accounting and systems ever needed in their remoter areas. But among the chiefs we ventured out singly and preserved the individuality of our

Token Woman: The One That Got Away

respective disciplines, never feeling that our personal identity was being submerged under the weight of a structure. Our only contract, throughout our work together, was commitment to our common ideals.

Always breaking new ground in the chiefs' use of computers to support their decision making, to enhance their control, our projects never became repetitive, except for the pressured period of our month-end reporting. But even these exercises frequently resulted in various ad hoc analyses. Despite our small number, our diversity gave us breadth to cover the infinite variety of circumstance that meets a cutting edge and throws the compound machinery of hierarchy into disarray. Our adversaries had no hope of anticipating our whims, our extreme flex and scope, all the possibilities generated by independent operatives. But there was no doubt in any mind that we were a team. And when the senior chiefs approved a mini of our own, we felt our strategies had been validated and expected the next stage of departmenthood and titles to follow in due time. With those acknowledgements of our contribution to the company's performance, we hoped that they would be receptive to the changes in our world that we wanted dearly. We would even have traded some of the perks that the men prized for ones important to us. That day and those visions seemed just over the horizon.

Chapter Ten
Bayesian Underwriting and Commercial Fires

Our sibling organization in the States to the South was experiencing a problem in their commercial underwriting. It was said that mobility and rising expectations were depleting their pool of knowledgeable underwriting staff. The situation was particularly acute for their commercial risks. These risks required a highly seasoned underwriter, someone who had been exposed to a broad range of businesses, from retail stores to manufacturing to storage facilities; someone who knew the basic construction techniques of typical physical plants; someone who could assess a company's basic financial health; someone who had accumulated a mental database of accidents and their causes; someone who could put all these pieces together into a gut-feel about a prospective insured's level of risk compared to others in their class. Now we knew that these skills required many years, broad exposures and much insight to develop. Our indians relied on long apprenticeships filled

Token Woman: The One That Got Away

with observation, and access to senior sages, to reach this level of proficiency in measuring our risks. Some called it 'sitting by Nelly', one of KGH's favorite analogies.

Although the Southern tribes were glutted with vice-presidents and fancy titles, their research resources were enviable and they were now planning a major assault on their underwriting difficulties. They hoped to capture the thought processes of their senior sages and use this expertise to improve the underwriting results of their junior staff. For this venture they were allocating major amounts of time and money in a process involving conferences and consultants, computers and controversial theories. Our chiefs expected that the real cause of their problems was inflated hype and an unwholesome taste for self-flagelation. But inflation had come to Canada and we were seeing rising attrition among our branches' junior staff, so our chiefs were open to observing what our Southern sibling would try. Being esoteric, it became our group's mission. The funding for our participation however was severely constrained. We would be allowed occasional visits only, not massive amounts of consultants' time nor many extended conferences with dozens of senior underwriters from around the country. That was Southern style.

This clearly very limited objective however held little benefit for our cause. Our scheme was to build an actual prototype of the expert system on our mini, with enhancements

Bayesian Underwriting & Commercial Fires

of our choosing and without waiting to see the Southerners' final solution. This ambitious project, originally code named C.A.R.E. for Computer Assisted Risk Evaluator, we christened Nelly. For our female sage, our Nelly, civility would be second nature; and we also planned to incorporate an automated version of the underwriting manual for commercial fire. This volume was a huge compendium of rules, standards, codes, instructions, exceptions. Comprehensive and intimidating, this resource, though vital to the underwriters, not only was a daunting challenge to the junior staff but was frequently in need of updates. Those replacement pages and additions issued by the chiefs did not always reach their intended destination in each and every copy of the book. A central automated version of the manual would be more manageable for both chiefs and indians. Although our prototype would only test the guidance function for our indians, the benefits of having to keep only our one final mainframe version current would make life simpler for the chiefs.

By integrating the manual with an expert system that emulated the thought processes of a senior chief as he combined the required assessments into a rating and then calculated the company's available capacity, of all kinds, our own and reinsurers, Nelly would make expertise more available to each indian while relieving the sages to concentrate their consultations on finer points. The junior staff could easily ask

Token Woman: The One That Got Away

Nelly hypothetical questions or what difference it would make if some borderline assessment had been different, which would tell him whether it was important to investigate further. To complete the package, our indians could send their results to print, eliminating transcription errors as they documented their work for the underwriting files.

We were excited at the promise this project held for the company. Our unwashed irregulars' approach held more benefit and was orders of magnitude less costly. After considering the Bayesian basis, I felt sure that I could take this on, even though the concept of a computer emulating an expert's thought processes was new and controversial. KGH took pains to reassure the systems tribe that we had no designs on their territory. Overextended, they were feeling more than a little unappreciative of suggestions that would complicate their lives. We knew the actuaries, in order to reduce their computer expenses, were attempting to establish themselves with access to the systems tribes' mainframe. Although the systems chief, Mullaly, was wary of more intruders, the impact of our eventual need for mainframe access, was not imminent. Since his tribe was preoccupied with accounting's tank operation for yet an extended time and the prototype concept did not excite them, they gave us no problem.

The Bayesian basis was not quite as simple as the usual textbook presentation. In principle, Bayes is a formula for

Bayesian Underwriting & Commercial Fires

reversing the relationship between clue and result, exactly what our sages required. In the sages' accumulated experience, they see the frequency of clues in their population of accidents but to underwrite a prospective insured they need the frequency of accidents given the presence of the clues. Basic Bayes says that the missing piece, the key to reversal, is the frequency of the clues in the general population. This information our sages draw from their knowledge of the marketplace.

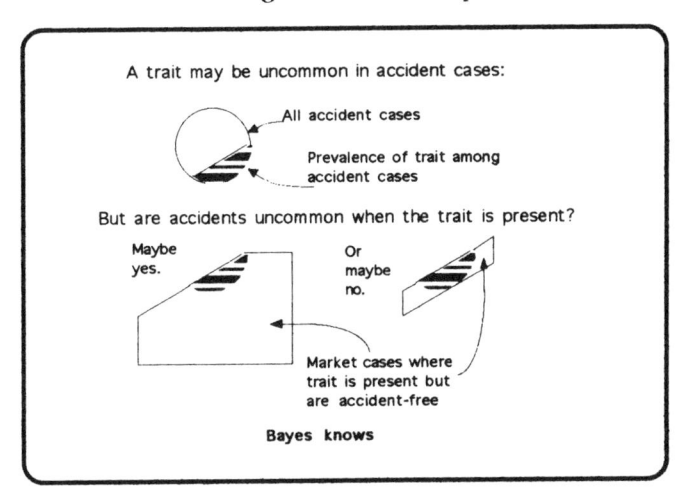

A trait may be uncommon in accident cases:
All accident cases
Prevalence of trait among accident cases

But are accidents uncommon when the trait is present?
Maybe yes.
Or maybe no.
Market cases where trait is present but are accident-free

Bayes knows

The complications come when there are clues of different natures not all predicting the same level of risk; clues based on distinct factors to be assessed, which was the case in underwriting. Some clues might be mildly worrisome, some ominous but different, some favorable in other aspects. Then

111

Token Woman: The One That Got Away

interactions become a consideration making the application of this concept strictly hair-raising. When my analysis of its theoretical validity ran into the need for independence of our factors, the Southern consultants suggested a visit to their headquarters in the land of Pentagon Chiefs.

The world there was all war-room dazzle with many banks of monitors, electronic shielding of whole rooms and a graphics department straight from Disney. Information on independence however was curiously scarce and I wondered more what my security clearance file contained. So in the end, we relied on common sense and empirical tests to determine whether the assumption of independence of our underwriting factors was a sufficiently reasonable approximation, at least for a starting point. When a history of usage was finally available, we planned to monitor outcomes so that Nelly's education would continue, adjust to change and improve. Our sages' confirmation that Nelly handled live examples to their expectations concluded our empirical testing.

We all learned many things and when the senior chiefs wanted us to take the major segment of the annual Branch Managers' Conference, we staged our own war-room show to introduce Nelly. Complete with banks of monitors, it was a big success. The performance of our prototype brought the senior chiefs visions of Nelly on the mainframe and Nelly's further education for many other commercial risks.

This was gratifying in its way but it brought us into conflict with the much larger systems tribe. They were loathe to undertake such a radically different burden. Mathematical programming was so much more complex and flexible than the standard business languages in use at that time, we were reluctant to relinquish new development, including Nelly's education. The language we had chosen was much better suited to a growing, learning entity and if systems took responsibility for Nelly they would likely start from scratch, reinventing the wheel using their own language.

In the end, we were given the mandate for Nelly's conversion and further education even though the full extent of such a task was far beyond our numbers. We concentrated on converting Nelly to live on the mainframe with its different operating system. Then we began to research Commercial Auto. These negotiations seemed to leave some spectre of our tribe being moved to systems territory, a possibility I found abhorrent because it would have taken us out of daily contact with the chiefs. Curiously it was one that seemed more real to KGH than to me. Though Nelly did make her new home in the big world of our branches' computer systems, it was not long afterwards that new opportunities made it necessary to defer Nelly's further development, effectively abandoning the remainder of the plan.

In the interim, we had a serious setback that led me to

Token Woman: The One That Got Away

reconsider our entire foundation. It began well enough. The senior chiefs acknowledged our work with raises, promotions and our coveted department name, Operations Research. In addition, the actuaries were to report to KGH, his future among the senior chiefs assured. But for his unwashed irregulars, there were details of our titles and job definitions that were in dispute. Ken returned from meetings with personnel, saying he had been blindsided and when he had risen to the fight he had been unable to make them see their error.

Personnel's new science was being invoked with such irony and treachery that we could only hope to expose the flaw in its foundation with time. They claimed they were describing our positions, not the incumbents of those positions. What assets an individual brought to the job were irrelevant, in essence claiming that they knew better than the incumbent what was needed, that the individual did not develop the position or enable the company to thrive in ways other incumbents would not imagine. Personnel and their consultants invented a list of abilities and assigned values in such a way that downplayed or ignored the abilities that we possessed. What hurt the most was the thought that we had supported these chiefs with such devotion, with such acknowledged performance. To accept that these chiefs could fail to come to their senses and repudiate this phony logic would open the door to madness.

Bayesian Underwriting & Commercial Fires

I could not completely hide the fact that I was disappointed at their refusal to acknowledge that my work required the creativity to handle the unexpected needs of a new science, just like the work required of a Ph.D. candidate. I was sure they would undo this absurdity once they had time to absorb the implications of this strange change in attitude, making the supposed position more important than the incumbent.

The only question was how long. The outer limit would not extend beyond when KGH became CEO, but that could be yet a while since our senior chiefs, Greer and Saville, did not seem close to their retirement. I had to believe that they would eventually see the fallacy. Surely our impact, our assets, were as significant as the actuaries whose traditional destination, even in our own Home Office, was the glorious number one spot. It was just a matter of continuing to demonstrate our merits. Opportunity soon knocked again.

Token Woman: The One That Got Away

Chapter Eleven
Mathematical Models or My Kingdom for a Lotus

The specialized mathematical models that we had built for our many diverse projects were beginning to cover every aspect of our operation and the impulse to connect them into one grand comprehensive construct was irresistible to any dreamer of castles. In our lunchtime scheming, KGH had been sketching coming crises and rumors of fears in the market. The outlines of the missing towers and moats, together with strategies of their use, were taking shape.

We would only need to add modules to produce estimates of expense and investment income. Those would complete our picture of the company's status. The links to connect these modules to our main models, Crystalball for exposures and Houdini for claims behavior, already existed. When the technical details of the programming connections were tested and assembled, we would hope for a balance of robustness and sensitivity.

116

Mathematical Models or My Kingdom for a Lotus

Because of the growth capacity inherent in accounting's computerization, the expense module could be built around the written policy count using incremental rates and staff productivities. Acquisition costs could be treated as a spinoff from the same policy count along with the premium rates, the two mainsprings of our exposure model. Investment income that flowed from the unearned premium reserves, specifically the use of premium funds until related claims occurred and were reported for payment, could be based on the complement of our exposure calculations of earned premiums; the arrival of claims being, in a sense, the earning of our premium and the end of its initial availability for investment. This part of our investment income, as well as the expenses, acquisition costs, and the premiums themselves would flow to the bottom line at the appropriate points in time. The earned exposures would flow to the claims model on their own timetable.

The claims model would then produce the tables of simulated, reported claims, their payment histories, their reserves and their so-called runoff, that excess over, or shortfall from, those reserves as the claims settled over time. The remaining part of investment income, that part arising from the use of moneys held for the eventual payment of reported claims, could be simulated from the tables of reserves generated by our claims model. This component of the investment income along with the claims' impacts then flowed

Token Woman: The One That Got Away

to the bottom line at their appointed times.

The whole structure would only require input about the rates, the resulting policy counts and projections of claims count per policy. Elegantly manageable. But before we would ask this grand model to draw the picture of the company's future bottom line emerging from choices of these few considered inputs, there would be a wealth of parameters to fine tune, such as various inflation rates, commission rates, interest rates, staff productivity. We would need to know what size changes in each of these parameters, or combinations of them, made substantive changes in the company future. If any proved sensitive, they would need to be treated as variable rather than parameter.

Because of the myriad delays inherent in the claims model, identifying the possible impact of any combination of input variables on the future would require an examination of the bottom line over an extended time frame. Our resulting picture of net status would need to be a sequence of yearends in order to describe the full impact of a given combination of rate strategy and market reaction. The perfect summary values to decorate the ends of a decision tree's branches!

As we put this model through testing, it exhibited such realistic behavior as we flexed its inputs and parameters, that it was more orrery; too mobile to envision it as stolid structure. It was sheer pleasure to watch it perform. To seek its insights

Mathematical Models or My Kingdom for a Lotus

was to approach a soothsayer and we so christened it. Our Oracle would be Houdini with a Crystalball, in a Pear Tree.

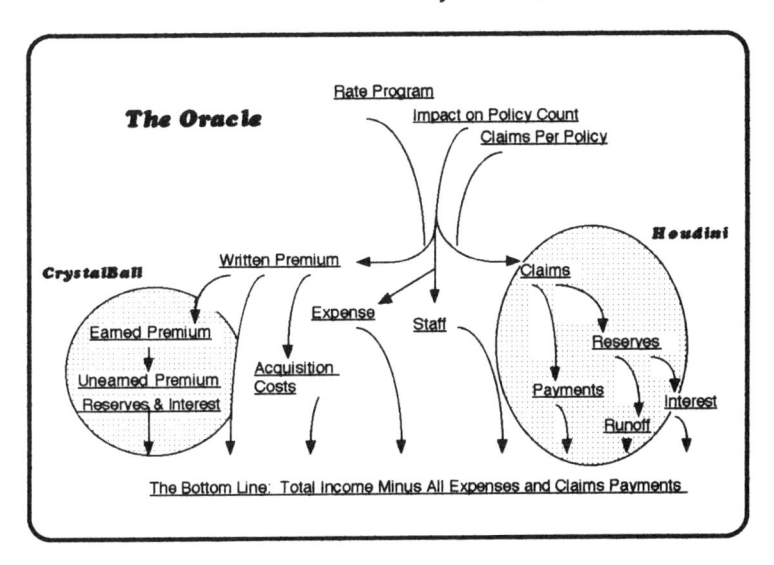

The Oracle

Houdini

CrystalBall

Rate Program
Impact on Policy Count
Claims Per Policy

Written Premium
Claims
Expense
Staff
Reserves
Earned Premium
Acquisition Costs
Payments
Interest
Unearned Premium Reserves & Interest
Runoff

The Bottom Line: Total Income Minus All Expenses and Claims Payments

Rumors of our successes had been entertaining Home Office for some time now and, in spite of our titles, London summoned us for an audience with their chiefs to see what we provincials were like, to see for themselves what magic we possessed, that they had found nowhere else. Not only were our systems, models and techniques very exciting but the tools we had at our disposal were the rough leading edge of technology and esoteric new languages; no such creatures yet as spreadsheets or modeling systems.

We had a couple of months to prepare our exhibits, to

Token Woman: The One That Got Away

gather our programs, to pack our bags and still when the days grew short there were surprises. The silliest of these was my last minute realization that I needed a passport. Britain didn't feel foreign to me, any more than Canada had those years ago. I looked forward to this first trip abroad because of those we were to meet, those I felt sure would strengthen our hand because they understood the level of skills in our work.

A passport was not the only legal document I was pursuing in those days. I told no one, but had been to see a sympathetic divorce lawyer because Isaac's storms were getting worse, not better. The affluence I had hoped would relieve our pressures seemed to buy only things, no matter how judiciously nor how lightly we handled it. And though Mary and Nermin and I shared many secrets, there were none outside who knew, though there was one day I nearly gave it away to KGH. It was during one of our quieter lunches and he had described his daughter's trauma in observing psychological violence at a friend's house. The puzzle of her terror baffled him but it struck deep chords in my soul and when I drew the picture clearer for him, with more feeling than I'd intended, I froze at how close I'd come to revealing my own terror.

The lawyer had bad news. My alarm over how close Isaac's temper was now coming to Michael made me consider these steps so long delayed, but the laws made it clear that my best chance of protecting Michael was by staying in the

Mathematical Models or My Kingdom for a Lotus

marriage. And so I closed that door and wondered what other defense I could find and how long I had to look. Something would come to me. There was always a way.

At the airport the royal treatment of a summons to London began and never faltered. It was first class all the way and our anticipation of finding allies filled my head with visions of centerstage without the fright. This pleasant paranoia climbed steeply when we stepped off the plane and were greeted by billboards, everywhere we turned, asking 'Who shot JR'. Me? JR was my way of signing memos, but it obviously couldn't be referring to me. It had to be those runaway visions of centerstage, that wild excitement while trying to be cool. Not being one of those inclined to notice soaps, my wide eyes had no explanation for this media blitz, just released, but I was loathe to ask and give it all away.

The Southerners had not totally overwhelmed the natives. I found many curious listings for TV shows that fondly covered working dogs and the fine distinctions of social class. And London's strange cabs all circled Trafalgar no matter where we went. And truly ancient little buildings, their structures badly skewed, were incongruously lodged between tall moderns. What puzzled me most and earned me my 'Yankee' badge was the observation that they weren't preserved, they were in use!

Day by day we did our show-and-tell to a receptive group. By night, they offered us limos, fine dining, and the best

Token Woman: The One That Got Away

tickets. Such wonderful choices in music held such emotional land mines and I stepped fully in. On the night we went to see the London stage version of Evita, we had spent an elegant dinner discussing the day's presentations. All was still going like clockwork and I was very pleased though our host's proud mention during one session that women were now admitted to the executive dining room had left me uneasy. But it was the musical that set off the fireworks. Or more precisely, the waterworks. I'd never been especially emotional about theater and I was caught totally off-guard when the complete futility of Evita's climb to the pinnacle of her society left me sobbing. At the door to my hotel room, KGH asked so tenderly if I was now recovered and though I wanted desperately to be held, I could never consider revealing my true feelings because, even if they would have been returned, I was sure neither of us would ever choose to be unfaithful. That night I simply cried to exhaustion. By the time we left, success had shown itself empty and I had decided to make one last try with Isaac.

Back at the office, the actuaries were growing restive. They were preparing to mount an offensive to pressure the senior chiefs to raise our auto rates, substantially. In many other places, the actuaries hold the reins and ours, it seemed, were so intent. KGH had many times consulted with our Oracle in test and would not support their move. Yet opposing it before they played their hand held no reward. He chose instead to

Mathematical Models or My Kingdom for a Lotus

nod and warn them of opposition among the market tribes, who would insist the price of being right was suicide. We would play our part by feigning weakness. And so we launched a project to convert the planning process to use a misbegotten language on the mainframe and continued to wind down our education of Nelly.

Late in the fall, when decision time was short, they made their move and when the lines were drawn, Operations Research again rode to the rescue of our chiefs. The lines separated two camps; those who favored the large increase demanded by the actuaries on the premise that claims trends would continue to worsen, and those who opposed increases now for political and marketing reasons.

The actuarial camp insisted that industry underwriting results were on the verge of going sour. They contended that by next May when those dire collective results would be published, the industry would be forced to raise their rates to levels likely similar to those our actuary advocated.

The marketing camp held that many of our competitors were convinced that, even if the results went sour, the trends would moderate by May. But, more importantly, if we adopted the actuary's rates now, we would lose so much of our portfolio of business due for renewal during the spring's seasonal surge that being right in May would be a Pyrrhic victory.

The actuary countered that it could easily be as

Token Woman: The One That Got Away

Pyrrhic, long term, to write the massive amounts of spring's business at grossly inadequate rates, since, by law, we were forbidden to raise rates to make up for bad past business. New rates may only pay for the losses associated with the new business to which the rates applied.

Unveiling Oracle, we began to draw the pictures that each side was describing so that all could see the true relative size and timing of each component's emergence. Freed from the need to deny opponents' realities, able to query details of each picture so they could assess even the non-quantifiable impacts of their proposals, and focussing on confirming the parameters they had contributed when we had consulted their expertise during development of Oracle, the chiefs shaped another plan as an alternative to the actuary's deadlock.

The consensus that industry underwriting results were about to go sour seemed firm ground; as was the fact that our company held a position, felt a responsibility for, industry leadership. The alternative plan was to raise rates by a moderate amount now, on the premise that our action as market leaders would encourage the more timid to follow suit rather than choose to suffer the poor underwriting results until May. We would take the loss of business now while the segment of our portfolio at risk was small. As the others adjusted their rates to preserve profitability, our rates would again be competitive in time for the spring season.

Mathematical Models or My Kingdom for a Lotus

With those two plans to choose from, with the eventual revelation of dire or not-so-dire claim trends, with the likely market responses and corrective actions, the decision tree took shape for Oracle's evaluation. The chiefs focussed on identifying the ranges of possibilities, from their worst case fears to the best they dared hope for, as well as most reasonable versions.

The Oracle returned detailed pictures of the outcomes of each of their scenarios, complete with sensitivities identified and short-term premonitions in a form ideal to monitor. Our fire brigade efficiency gave them all they asked, within the time they needed. Their decision was their own.

They chose to lead the market with a more moderate increase and bravely hoped the competition, still cowering from memories of government intervention, would rouse themselves from bygone fears and follow, before the major wave of spring business swept ashore. But they would not go blind into this fray. We were set for monitoring and knew the last moment at which our ship could turn before the spring wave. It was a narrow window in February between our last monitoring data's availability and the action date, during which we would have to reassess our options, some as yet unknown, if our ship needed turning.

We put the new rates in place and the days seemed longer though fall had not yet changed to winter. Our work

Token Woman: The One That Got Away

had put the electricity in the air but at the grand Christmas ball, Nermin and Mary were not among our worthy braves. And I wished I wasn't, when the door prize had my name on it and Santa expressed his wish. Clearly, Santa would never have asked any other chief for a little kiss as he presented the prize, but the night was filled with Hollywood glamour, where kisses are exchanged so lightly. Yet this was a British formal occasion, not a more effusive romance culture. I blinked momentarily but the other alternatives that came to mind seemed ungracious, at the very least. I atoned for that graciousness by spending the prize on a grand department lunch.

December's results were yet clueless but the street noise was bad and so word was sent that January's branch managers' conference would focus on their best reconnaissance. The result was gloom and dread. There was a sense that January's numbers would be conclusive, so conclusive we needn't, in fact dare not, wait for final accuracy. So we sought them in the rough. Our worst case scenario for market response was confirmed and the fire brigade went into action again.

An emergency meeting of the Quebec and Ontario chiefs was called to assess what incentives would be needed to return the agents to our fold. Although the market had marginally shifted in the direction we had led, the agents considered our rates unacceptable. One possibility was to set our rates at the current market average, telling the independent agency forces

Mathematical Models or My Kingdom for a Lotus

that we would accede to their assessment even though we felt we would suffer major underwriting losses. Some among the market tribes insisted that agents had already formed habits of going to other insurers and we would need a substantive inducement to motivate their reform. As corrective actions were considered, they were built into Oracle's programming and new pictures emerged telling us the secret to success in dealing with the cowards in the market.

Rate modification, modification with incentive, and standing pat were the choices in the expanding decision tree taking shape. The short term result would unquestionably be an industry-wide blood-letting. In exploring these scenarios though, we discovered that the deepest initial abyss led to the ultimately best of the available outcomes. The secret was twofold. With a fixed expense floor, we could cover those expenses best by growth, because per policy costs would be minimized. To gain this growth in the short term with any degree of assurance, required the additional costs of the incentive, and Houdini's earlier success at defeating bureaucratic robbers still offered some cushion to finance them by keeping the initial abyss from being too prohibitive; too much of a certain loss to be worth a more remote, less certain, gain. We could afford to bleed better than our competitors and we would heal better and quicker. With some trepidation, the chiefs this time chose the most aggressive of our options and

Token Woman: The One That Got Away

presented it to all concerned. Succeeding in resolving their dilemma, all within the window of time needed to turn their ship, it was now a matter of time and monitoring.

Home Office not only had concurred but the big invitation arrived to the international underwriting conference in July and it had our names on it. But there was no word about titles and changes that mattered to us. We began developing our presentation and magically funds were available for professional bards and time for extended rehearsals.

The conference was held at a manor house near Canterbury in England. Michael sent me off with his good luck charm but I decided to keep the rabbit's news to myself. At the opening dinner, amid pomp and ceremony, the most senior of London's chiefs chose to be my escort and KGH's anxiety was palpable but unwarranted. Being the only woman participant at the conference, my hosts took pains to arrange private quarters in the main house rather than the more dormitory accommodations for the men with their pub-like gathering areas.

All the polish we'd invested in our preparation showed in our performance but KGH was curiously deferential about Canadian accomplishments with the other participants and they did not pursue any additional information from me on our work. At the closing dinner, many tributes and toasts were raised by the participants to celebrate and express their

Mathematical Models or My Kingdom for a Lotus

appreciation for many of the gifts brought from the far parts of the realm. It was so interesting to observe. Tasteful and clever until the American representative gave his list of uses for the company scarf which included substituting it for a brassiere. Relief was spelt H-O-M-E.

The presentation had been the conference jewel and when we returned home, an encore was demanded in the Boardroom. Our chiefs celebrated our success with an afternoon reception after our performance and many of them applauded us enthusiastically afterwards.

Token Woman: The One That Got Away

Chapter Twelve
All Good Things

With the applause still ringing in our ears, Mary and Nermin held visions of on-sight childcare to support our work when my baby was due and we celebrated the day I told KGH. The company, after all, offered many perks to improve the productivity of the chiefs. Feeling that we had demonstrated the significance of our contribution to the company's bottom line, it seemed the right time to feel out what KGH would think of our dreams. Our enthusiasm about our desire to have our children close by as we worked brought his smiles but no indication of any possibilities of company interest. In fact, the subject took on the air of pie in the sky so I made arrangements for my baby to stay at the on-site daycare center that City Hall had established for their employees. It would be close enough that I could spend my lunches there with my baby but the waiting list we were on was long. This was worrisome but worse was the fact that KGH began spending his lunches with the actuary. I wondered how Mary and Nermin would feel when they realized that this was becoming the usual situation. But I was already using my empty lunch calendar to prepare for my baby's arrival. Expectant mothers have a new joy to hide within.

The days until delivery were quiet. With careful planning, I expected to return to the office shortly after the baby was born. Feeling we really didn't need to rush to wind down my projects, the days seemed more leisurely as we continued to monitor the results of our last rescue mission for the chiefs. But one day, early on in my pregnancy, as I was peacefully working alone at lunchtime, I was gazing into space puzzling through some problem when, with a surge of delight, the most pleasant image of a beautiful little baby momentarily appeared in my line of vision. I considered the possibility that I had been daydreaming or that some memory had surfaced but the image did not match anything I could recall. It hadn't felt like a daydream, certainly not something I had engineered; in fact, I had felt so elated to see this baby. I discounted the possibility of an hallucination, since I had no sense of anything wrong, no connection. I decided that it must have been my imagination. Being an atheist at the time, I had no way of explaining it or even discussing it but now I think that I was experiencing my own personal epiphany.

I took my leave when the baby arrived, wanting to be

Token Woman: The One That Got Away

back soon, for Mary and Nermin's sake because we were a team and I would miss them. But this was not to be. The problems began and my return was delayed, again and again. While I was out, my ever-resourceful friends inadvertently gained access to confidential information.

The day that I made the emergency trip into the office, I was feeling very apprehensive after Mary's phone call. In fact, since coming home from the hospital, I had been feeling despondent at the thought of having to leave my daughter. It seemed she could sense my feelings. She didn't even want to go out for a walk regardless of the weather. I wasn't sure that we would make it to the subway, but we did. I thought that if she made a commotion at the office that we could just close the department door. That was the only way I could imagine even taking her and it was my only choice. My daycare arrangements had fallen through even though I had made them as soon as I knew I was pregnant. My only other choice had been to hire a nanny but she hadn't arrived yet. While we were waiting for her to come, I had to arrange our move to a townhouse further from the subway because it was the only solution to all the problems that piled up the day my daughter was born. Isaac wanted a British-trained nanny and that was also when he finally decided that he wanted to have his own business. His plan was to sell our condo and use the money to invest in his venture. I didn't want to move, especially with a new baby, so I resisted, but when my daycare arrangements fell through and we needed more space for the nanny, I finally gave in. These changes were all making our expenses go up so there was no chance to change my mind. I would have to go back to work even though I couldn't bear to leave her. I had delayed it as long as I could but that dreaded day was almost there.

Mary had said that she and Nermin were hoping that I could help them understand something they'd found at the photocopier. Even though she didn't say exactly what it was, it seemed to be quite urgent. When we had exchanged greetings and exhausted all the news, that's when they took a file from the back of one of the drawers. As I studied the contents of these papers, the one that seemed the most explicit was the chart that claimed to be the payscales of the systems tribe. The thing that struck me was the progression.

As you moved up from level to level, the salaries rose by a constant factor, making this scale rise exponentially because when numbers increase by a fixed percentage reapplied at each stepup, the further up the scale you go the larger each step becomes, making the top unimaginable. Since the scales for the company were determined by personnel, there was no escaping the conclusion that the senior chiefs had been seduced into adopting personnel's new science for either greed or ego. When you imagine that your salary in someway measures your worth to the company, claiming that they were exponentially

Token Woman: The One That Got Away

worth more than their indians said that our senior chiefs no longer considered any of us as assets. Realizing that there was only a limited pot to divide up, the senior chiefs couldn't help but know that they were taking food from the mouths of our children.

Since the bottom of the scale was where the women in the company were, the idea that we were working our way up and that the company was not afraid to consider us equals was simply absurd. The number of levels we would have to climb to reach the titles we felt were appropriate, would have taken a lifetime. When could we end the sacrifice of our children? Those unwilling to share the decision making could simply add more layers to the middle management, making our climb that much more difficult. In fact, with personnel's exponential formula for greed, the senior chiefs even had incentive to do exactly that, all the while protected by the appearance of 'science' and concern for equity. All just propaganda. It became clear that they only considered us payroll expenses. That's when I remembered the payslip incident. It had to have been that their concern was the fear that someone noticing just how low my pay had been might have inadvertently made a comment which could have become a source of unrest. It was inescapable. Then the incident in college, when it had been apparent that protesting would have been futile, came to mind.

Making an issue out of this hypocrisy would not have

endeared us to personnel or the senior chiefs and, on recommendations, when we later needed to seek employment elsewhere, we were likely to be labeled malcontent. The realization that this new personnel 'science' was beginning to be adopted more widely, and probably for the same reasons, meant that, even if I succeeded in climbing some corporate ladder, the powers-that-be would never do more than create positions for token women with no real power. Worst of all, in the process of getting there, complicity with this formula for greed would eventually seem more natural.

As the full implication of these scales sank into our consciousnesses, our usual tempo of exchanges slowed to a standstill. Words could not convey the vision of what we would need to do. Our only alternative was to do what all good unwashed irregulars do before their spirits are totally broken. They slip, one-by-one, into the night and find their way home until their spirits heal and move them to start a new life. Distracted, each wandered back to their own private thoughts, knowing that the others of us would understand whatever it was that they would choose to do.

Nermin was the first to succeed in making her exit. Though she didn't move that far, it took more courage. She went to KGH and raised the issue of her stalled career. When KGH could not offer her anything in Operations Research, his only alternative was to suggest lateral moves to improve her

Token Woman: The One That Got Away

chances later. She accepted an opening on the other side of the corporate pyramid because, now that the company consisted of positions and not indians, that was what the company had become. A collection of pyramids built for a pharaoh and his privileged elite. When I spoke to KGH later about Nermin's departure, there was no indication that he suspected. He just thought she would do well in her new position.

By the time I returned, Mary had found her own future. She and her children were leaving to join her sister who was starting her own bush pilot operation in the land of oil and opportunity. When I was contacted for an assessment of her abilities as a junior programmer, I was so overwhelmed with my own difficulties in moving to a new home that I never did solve my dilemma. Mary's forays into programming had been recent and her progress limited. I felt it was, at best, too soon to tell but now it was important. Should I reveal my doubts about her progress? Would it be more cruel to discourage her, risking the infamous self-fulfilling prophecy? Or was it more cruel to encourage her when my own doubts could be the confirmation she needed to avoid embarrassment or the realization later of wasted years, wasted hard work? Maybe even lost chances because Mary had many other talents. There was a cruel danger either way. I opted to give her a glowing recommendation when she needed it and wished her all the best. My sorrow at my inability to do better added to my

All Good Things

growing despondency, knowing that, if I had chosen wrong, I wouldn't be there to even explain, console, to ask forgiveness. Then I set aside this heinous task of judging another's ability, hoping that someday I would see her again, my friend, and first ally.

My own exit took somewhat longer. It was not so simple. Trying to manage with a new baby and an increased workload, I didn't see how I could continue. Before I could even imagine what I could do, I discovered that Isaac had made a serious error in judgment, one that cleared a safe path through the legal tangles of Canadian domestic courts. With that one stroke of his pen, the turmoil of our relationship could be relieved, if I could convince myself that it was really possible to carry the entire complicated operation through. It was too opportune, too much of a gift from the Universe to ignore.

When the nanny also proved unreliable, my family began to make more frequent visits in an effort to tide us over, making their help available as best they could. Otherwise I think I would have lost my mind. Two days before the end, I finally revealed my plan to KGH. Even though my heart was aching to explain or even to ask, I only told of my own personal troubles, knowing that our strategy of attachment and concealment, as his protege, would be a danger to him if he even suspected the full extent of my treason. But since our tribe had become an expense and not an asset to the company, I harboured

Token Woman: The One That Got Away

only one shadow of guilt, knowing that our future together could have been so significant if the senior chiefs had not been seduced by Personnel's hypocrisy. Since there now was no honorable alternative, I finally knew that I could do it.

Intently studying the emptiness of our department, KGH's last comment was that he had thought he had seen a glimpse of my terror the day he had described his daughter's reaction to a domestic violence scene and he wondered at the time if I had been hiding something. Perhaps he was somehow asking if I was hiding something again but I doubt it. I don't think he ever guessed. He gave me leave to pack my things and finish the details of my plan with time on my side. My nerves were shot but somehow we carried off the act. The morning Isaac left on a business trip, the movers came and we stepped through the door and across the border to home in the South.

I love my daughter. She is so dear to me and I never could have done it without her. She was the one who saved me from becoming involved any more deeply in the personnel tribe's own uncleanness. You see, it had not been long before, that I had learned my own tribe's abysmal salaries. Administration had not been one of my responsibilities as office wife. Unrealistically hoping that things would change, it was now inertia that kept me going. She convinced me that stubborn persistence was just futile. She was my Last Straw.

Hello Damon, it's Pythias

While we tread the miles of our quest
I was your companion, your ego's mate.
We were invincible it seemed and never missed.
Astaire and Rogers, they said, the show was all.
Yours the sketch, the vision, the grand concept.
Mine the footwork, the turns, the magic as we shook it out.

I wielded matrix and vector, function and string,
to justify your faith, to build your fortresses,
to see your eyes shining for me.
You hosted our party royally planned,
sharing the wealth of your mind's eye,
daring the world's sideways glance.

But they held success against us.
Its essence must be canned, defined its K's and A's.
Corporate assets turned to paper dust.
Describe the position, not the person, the experts said.
Your anger met the science icy and deformed.
Heavy handed, they crushed the intuition that fed them,
substituting shame and doubt, solidarity dying last.

When the strange new days came, your faith gone,
you turned away, no more invulnerable to the glance.
Invisible, I was alone, and the walls of our house,
with all inside, turned to ash.
Each, in turn, we took our leave
til only our positions remained,
for fit monument to my Damon's demise; for now
no person, no model, no tree, no joy survives.

Goodbye Damon, your unknowing Pythias returned too late.

Afterword

To our daughters making their career choices..

The educational system, with its connections to industry, as well as simple inertia, is set to sweep you into the corporate world. Many of you, because of intuition or because of your innate commitment to ideals, are wary of that bargain. If your mothers and older sisters ventured down that path, they will tell you that it won't be as hard as their experience; at least you won't be alone.

Many women in leadership positions will be cheering you on from the sidelines, tabulating their successes as you take each step along that path and reporting to any who will listen. There have been questionable tactical decisions made in the name of the parity objective, both in science careers, and in the academic market, willfully exaggerating their promise. But the cheering is seductive.

Nurture the reluctance that lingers in your mind. In that back corner, you sense that, even though your education is giving you a clearer picture of your special skills and interests, you are being asked now to knowingly buy into a bad bargain; that you will have to work harder than your male peers to stay even, that you will be paid less than is fair, that your chance of facing divorce court is high, that your chance of losing custody of your children will increase markedly in this deal and that the stresses will increase your likelihood of succumbing to disease.

Is parity just over the horizon or is it more likely we can't even get there going in this direction? The vaulted progress, in monetary, status or lifestyle terms, is so meager. Ten cents and glass ceilings, for over twenty years valiant efforts! And what key information did the Labor Department project? The job market will continue to be highly unstable. You can expect to need to change employers several times in your career, for the corporation's supposed benefit. The likelihood of so-called family friendly initiatives making any more headway in that environment is vanishingly small. Progress in millimeters is proof of the impotence of this strategy.

Some will tell you this is progress, realistic progress, but is that enough justification to balance against such a deal so detrimental to your happiness and eventually to your own children's well-being? Aren't you really being used as 'cannon-fodder'? Is the corporate equity strategy the best life has to offer? It is not your only choice.

Surveying a raft of resources on women's experiences over the last twenty years, you will find, though you will have to draw your own conclusions since vested interests have reframed this problem as 'coping with daycare', that the only women who have succeeded in combining successful careers and satisfying rearing of their children have been those who were casually self-employed. The corollary to that conclusion is that this is the direction towards which we should be moving heaven and earth to find you, and ourselves, a viable route.

Several million women are already started on this route, with informal networks growing day-by-day. The volume of the 'job-route' may seem overwhelming since the corporate world controls media and the major publishing venues. Meanwhile, they and their unwitting supporters, their greed and their hype, are relentlessly driving us down the path to ecological, personal, cultural as well as economic collapse and you?.. you are expected to supply the muscle, the labor (cheaply, at that), the blood, sweat and tears to power their blueprint. Women started a proud tradition of effective, radical, sensible opposition to insanity in power centers, national and international, with the Women's Strike for Peace, without major funding, without cumbersome organization. We can do it again.

We need no funding, no approval to launch this. Within four years, as your generation comes through university level preparation and enters the marketplace with women's networking support, we could turn our destinies around. No more begging for dimes per sacrificed generation! With an auxiliary plan to enable my own generation to leave the corporate world in larger numbers, we could consider this a genuine revolution.

The leverage potential could be phenomenal, creating our own alternative economy and social structure that responds to the dreams women went into the workworld to make real. In fact, it's exactly those unfulfilled dreams that could supply many of the business plans we will need. The more of us who put the word out, help develop the idea, form the networks and commitments, the more smooth and rapid will be our revolution. On the internet, in our writing, by fax, we can exchange ideas on tactics, the dimensions of this strategy, its implications. Today, let's begin today to think of ourselves as creators of our own work, our own realm.

To my corporate sisters..

Many of you are already thinking of abandoning the careers you now pursue but are reluctant to go against the tide of institutionally-abetted thinking with its foregone conclusion that, short of declaring defeat, you will continue to struggle for each inch even though the inches gained are lost in the shellgames that define our well-being as well as our economic status. This book is for you too.

When your resolve to try something new and different is being overwhelmed by fatigue and that ingrained need to feel that all we've done wasn't wasted, pick up your copy of <u>Token Woman</u> and remember that your life from this day forward is worth more than twenty years of vanishing inches. It will remind you that you can go your own way and genuinely win. Pulling out is not abandoning your ideals nor your sisters. In fact, your act of pulling out and joining pioneers of a new direction will ease your sisters' ultimate transitions and make it possible to live the ideals you had hoped would influence the corporate world when you joined, expecting a woman's touch to make its mark there. More than that. Your escape can have an impact on the corporate juggernaut. They don't realize it yet but we don't need them as much as they need us. The reason is basically population demographics, here and abroad.

The truth is that sooner or later the corporate world, with its obsessive pursuit of the gilded competitive edge, will run out of those to exploit. Top managements are in the midst of waging a war of their own creation and are oblivious to anything but their need to amass market share and endlessly strangle their corporate opponents. Their agenda defines customers as owners of income, which is to be made accessible through incessant, inescapable barrages of manipulative advertising; that agenda defines staff as an expense to be reduced as if it were waste. Is there hope that this scene will develop into a humane workplace? Token Woman reminds you that personnel smoothes the way for that top management to avoid thinking about what their actions do to Tiny Tim and focus instead on the fairmarket salary to pay for the limited function allotted to Bobbie Cratchett to perform, all the while padding the golden parachutes and justifying the inflated salaries of top management as the pinnacle of their conveniently engineered hierarchies. The dynamics of this world are unalterably stacked against your idealism and your mental well-being.

If the voices of public leaders in government agencies and educational institutions, whose intended portfolio is to protect you and promote your efforts, tell you to keep the faith, that your struggles were not rewarded because you needed more education, more credentials, better instincts, supportive mentors, more leverage, more chances to shine, Token Woman reminds you that this guilt-trip is unwarranted. And there are many other counterexamples, other token women we hope will be encouraged to come forward.

When you are told that we've come a long way but such cultural changes are naturally slow processes, Token Woman reminds you that your life and your family's lives are not statistics, not expendable entities to be allocated to the support of one particular offensive, one particular set of tactics. There are better ways to secure our freedom and our well-being.

One by one, we can seek those ways, keeping in touch with

our sisters who have already gone out on their own. Seeking to make our original ideals a reality, we can gain our well-being and establish the mechanisms and dynamics for our children's freedom. Come, make your plan, reach and find your place. Token Woman celebrates your coming out.

To the guys..

I hope you don't think you're outside our struggle. Your recent undoing by the corporate world is clear from the numbers. The robber barons are not your idols. The numbers show how they used you. Over the last twenty years, your average salary actually went down in spite of the enormous increases in the barons' take. Their cowardly performance when we came to their door left you, as well as us, vulnerable to the inevitable downsizing inherent in their pyramid-padding.

Nor is our strategy intended to be exclusive. We welcome more players. But you were sucked into the company store sooner and more securely so this time maybe it's our turn to ride to your rescue, to find a way for our children and our husbands to pursue the life's work that their hearts are into. If you think that's too maternalistic, relax, we expect you'll live up to your role as 'joy to women and children' as well as pulling your own weight. No different than you'd expect of us.

On the other hand should you tire of being right-sized and expendable, should you crave family, hearth or even just your own self-direction, know that we appreciate your struggle to be responsible.

So when you hear me called 'Stupid Girl', and you surely will, know that it's all right. That's what differentiates those who try from the 'smart ones' who unendingly weasel, who this time will go down with the robber-elite as they wage their terminal battles to exploit ever more remote parts of this world. The clock will run out on them and we will be on our feet, on our way home, exploring our new world...

To order additional copies of <u>Token Woman: The One That Got Away</u> simply copy the form below. Make checks payable to Dectiré Publishing. Send the form, filled in, with your check or credit authorization to:

        Dectiré Publishing
        P.O. Box 18242
        Fairfield, OH 45018-0242

Please send ___ copies ($11.95 per copy) of <u>Token Woman: The One That Got Away</u> to my address:

Name:_____

Address:_____

City/State/Zip:_____

Visa____ MC____

Card #_____ ExpDate_____

Signature_____

Please add 5.5% for books shipped to Ohio addresses. For shipping, book rate, add $2.00 for the first book and $.75 for each additional book.

___ Please add my name to the mailing list for <u>Last Straw Revolution</u>'s latest issue. I understand that it's my sample copy of the bi-monthly newsletter that keeps the ball in play with news and views on tactics, issues and answers. Featuring letters from pioneers and supporters, as well as articles on other pieces of our puzzle, it keeps its readers in touch with each other.

And last but not least, lest we become bottom-feeders, profiting from the misery of others, a major percentage of the proceeds of the sale of this book, after they determine that its legitimate expenses are paid, will be for groups and projects whose nature is consistent with the ideas this book expresses.